CREATIVE DRAMATICS

for children

Maureen McCurry Cresci

with the assistance of
Debra Gordon-Zaslow

Scott, Foresman and Company
Glenview, Illinois   London

Good Year Books
are available for preschool through grade 12 and for every basic curriculum subject plus many enrichment areas. For more Good Year Books, contact your local bookseller or educational dealer. For a complete catalog with information about other Good Year Books, please write:

Good Year Books
Department GYB
1900 East Lake Avenue
Glenview, Illinois 60025

To My Husband Sal
With many thanks to the following students who so willingly participated and made the creation of this book possible: Laura Collins, Mark Hardy, Sheri Johnson, Michelle Johnson, Rene Kipness, Darrell Seaman, and Wanda Wesley.

A very special thank you to Debra Gordon Zaslow of Ashland, Oregon, who did such wonderful work in extending the teacher's guidelines—and, of course, to my original and multi-talented teaching partner, Iris Rainer.

ISBN 0-673-38464-0

Contents

PART 1: LOSING INHIBITIONS AND LOOSENING UP   1

PART 2: LEARNING CONTROL   20

PART 3: SPEECH   27

Preface

The creative dramatic exercises in this book offer opportunities for children to develop acting skills and to express themselves in unique ways. Children are natural actors, and even the shyest ones will be drawn into the fun. While enjoying themselves, they'll explore and develop their own imaginations. They'll build self-confidence by being in front of a group, and they'll learn to be respectful of (and listen to) others. They'll not only express emotions but also learn how to control them. Finally, they'll develop greater degrees of concentration.

Creative Dramatics for Children provides an easy-to-follow and basic approach to leading simple and fun theatre games. It is a book written for teachers and group leaders interested in helping children express themselves through drama; the exercises have been used with students of all ages as well as with professional child actors.

Concluding each of the book's five parts are suggestions for extending the activities to other subject areas of the curriculum. These extension ideas increase the book's practicality for today's busy teachers, as they offer a creative and flexible way to make additional use of many of the exercises in the classroom.

The author would like to thank Anita Meinbach and Laura Fendel for their helpful reviews of the manuscript.

Using This Book in the Classroom

Creative Dramatics for Children is organized in five parts, each of which offers specific goals and suggestions for introducing the activities. Although the format makes it easy to locate specific types of activities, don't think that you must use the book in a linear fashion from start to finish. You can easily mix and match exercises to suit the needs of yourself and your students. For example, students who are already expressive and without inhibitions can skip many of the exercises in Part 1, while other students may need to repeat several Part 1 exercises before moving on. You must gauge what is appropriate for your students and how much to cover in each session.

Take some time to familiarize yourself with the scope of the book before doing any of the exercises. You may find that you want to include exercises from different parts in a single drama session. For example, you might start with a group imagery exercise, move on to a speech or improvisation exercise, and end with a relaxation or sensory awareness activity.

If you can't arrange a whole block of time for a drama session, consider using just one exercise at a time between subjects. Many of the short exercises that require mental focus are well-suited for transitions between subjects. During a gym class, for example, you might want to try some of the exercises that emphasize physical control; some of the more energetic, emotional-release exercises might be appropriate before a recess. You will soon get a sense of what works well for you and your students at different times in the day.

Basic Guidelines in Teaching Creative Dramatics

To enhance the effectiveness of all the exercises in this book, keep the following guidelines in mind:

Be familiar with and enthusiastic about the material.
Take the time to read and understand each exercise fully before presenting it to the children. Teachers who are comfortable and excited about an exercise find that the children will be also.

Give clear directions, but **do not** *offer examples.*
Explain the exercise as thoroughly as possible. Then allow the children to interpret it in their own way. Teacher-given examples have a strong tendency to block the creative flow of ideas.

Be willing to accept and appreciate all kinds of responses.
Remind the children that there is no right or wrong way to do the exercises. Some children may have a hard time grasping this concept, preferring to imitate the approach of other children. Gently urge such children to do the exercise their own way, and praise them for even the most modest attempts at a unique interpretation. Always give the children permission to act out their feelings, characters, and situations in the way that seems right to them.

Remind the children not to hurt one another.
Set physical limits from the start. For example, it's not unusual for children to think that it's permissible—when pretending to be large raindrops—to fall on top of each other! Tell them that while the exercises are lots of fun, they must keep within their own space for safety's sake.

Instruct the children to be respectful of and courteous to each other.
Let your students know that you expect them to pay attention to the person(s) performing. Make sure that each student has an opportunity to complete his or her performance before others become involved.

Using the Extension Activities

At the end of each part, you will find a section entitled "Extending the Activities into Other Areas of the Curriculum." This listing provides brief descriptions of optional activities for teachers who would like to integrate drama into other subject areas. The extension activities are divided into four major subject areas: writing, art, social studies, and science. Every drama exercise that has a correlated activity suggestion at the end of the part is designated by a symbol in the text:

Writing   **Art**   **Social Studies**   **Science**

Although not all of the correlated activities will match your particular subject goals, you may find many that suit your plans and your class. None of these optional activities, of course, is essential to teaching creative dramatics.

Ideally, the combination of drama exercises and extension activities will spark both your own and your students' creativity and make your classroom a more exciting and enjoyable place in which to learn!

PART 1
LOSING INHIBITIONS AND LOOSENING UP

Much of what we do in school requires linear, logical thinking. Creative drama requires just the opposite. Part 1 is designed to help students loosen up mentally and physically and to promote a creative flow of ideas.

The following exercises lay the foundation for all kinds of dramatic activity—speech, storytelling, skits, improvisations, plays, etc. They encourage both the sensory awareness necessary to good acting and the ability to call forth and express a wide variety of emotions. In addition, this part includes relaxation exercises which, while useful anytime, are particularly appropriate after some of the more energetic activities. Relaxation exercises can help calm and focus the group before moving on to another subject.

Introducing the Exercises to Your Students

Ask the children to close their eyes and recall any good actor or actress they have seen. Tell them to focus on what they thought was good about the acting. Explain that the qualities needed to be a good actor or actress don't always come naturally; most performers must train themselves to act well.

Discuss the specific goals of this part, and tell your students how the activities relate to these goals. Emphasize that the first five activities—dealing with group imagery—are not just for children. Although the activities are a lot of fun, professional actors and actresses of all ages take these exercises very seriously.

Group Imagery and Movement

The following five exercises are among the very few in this book in which the instructor should actually become physically involved with the group. If the leader is loose and uninhibited, the children will be also. When leading these exercises, take plenty of time to move from one suggestion to another.

These are group exercises for all age levels. Students act out their own interpretations of what the teacher is suggesting. Although you should encourage jumping, stomping, yelling, and laughing in these exercises, remind the children not to become physical with each other. These are wonderful exercises with which to end a class.

EXERCISE 1

From Specks of Dust to Feathers

We are all tiny specks of DUST . . . we are so small that no one can see us . . . we are floating around in the air outside . . . the wind is blowing us slowly through the air . . . we move very slowly . . . the wind just carries us along.

We land on a little LEAF in a stream . . . the stream carries us along . . . the water starts moving faster and faster . . . we are suddenly in a WHIRLPOOL . . . we are going around and around . . . we are going around in circles . . . faster and faster . . . all of a sudden the water throws us out onto the beach. We lie very still . . . we are very tired.

A SOFT WIND comes along and carries the leaf we are on to a BIG TUMBLEWEED . . . the tumbleweed is very large and round . . . the wind blows the tumbleweed around very slowly . . . the wind feels good . . . slowly blowing us around.

Now everyone has become a person with a pillow . . . we are all in a giant PILLOW FIGHT . . . we throw pillows hard at each other . . . we pick up pillows and throw them . . . harder and harder . . . faster and faster . . . all the pillows break at once and feathers fly all around us and we all fall down . . . exhausted. We lie there and watch the feathers come down from the sky. They feel so soft as they start to cover us. We lie there and relax.

EXERCISE 2

From Balloons to Popcorn

We are all BALLOONS in a bunch . . . we are at a circus . . . the man that is holding onto the strings lets go . . . we all fly up into the sky . . . we all go our separate ways . . . up, up into the sky . . . higher and higher . . . floating . . . going where the wind takes us . . . higher and higher.

We are still very high in the sky, but now we are people . . . people who can walk on clouds . . . we play with the clouds . . . we can jump from one to another . . . we jump . . . we lie down on them and roll around . . . we can push them together and make bigger places to play . . . we jump on the soft clouds.

We are now back down on Earth . . . we are in this very room . . . there is STICKY TAPE all over the floor . . . we are all trying to walk across the room . . . it is so hard to walk . . . every step that we take is so much effort . . . we have to walk all the way across the room.

The floor is not sticky anymore. The floor has become a giant sheet of RUBBER . . . every step makes us sink way down and way back up again . . . we can jump way up into the sky . . . we jump and jump and jump . . . we get so tired from jumping that we fall down on the floor.

We lie there a minute. What is happening now? The floor is getting hot. We have all become KERNELS OF CORN, and the floor is burning hot . . . in a few seconds we'll all explode into POPCORN . . . the floor is getting so hot that it makes us roll around . . . when we explode into popcorn we'll jump up and yell "POP" . . . hotter and hotter and hotter . . . we can't stand it anymore . . . get ready . . . hotter and hotter . . . get up . . . now . . . let's all "POP"!!

EXERCISE 3

From Caterpillars to Balloons

We are all big fuzzy caterpillars . . . crawling through the forest . . . we travel very slowly . . . it takes us a very long time to move along . . . we just creep.

We have now become MARBLES . . . we are rolling on the floor . . . we can't stop rolling . . . on the floor . . . we can't stop rolling . . . there are beautiful colors inside of us . . . the colors flash as we roll around

. . . we keep rolling and rolling . . . suddenly we stop.

We are all wadded up into tight little balls . . . we have all become very small FLOWER SEEDS . . . there is a soft rain falling on us . . . it makes us start to sprout . . . our legs are slowly becoming roots . . . the sun comes out and warms us all up . . . we start reaching for the sun . . . we slowly reach . . . we stand up and reach . . . we can feel all our flower buds start to open slowly . . . the sun feels so warm and we all slowly and gracefully become FLOWERS.

We stand and let the sun shine down on us. We have started to change again. We have all become big fat SNOWMEN . . . we are standing very proudly under the sun . . . the sun is starting to get hotter . . . we are very slowly starting to melt . . . the sun is hotter and hotter . . . slowly we are becoming very very small . . . we are all becoming PUDDLES OF WATER . . . the puddles are very still and quiet.

We aren't puddles anymore. Now we are BALLOONS with no air in them. Someone starts to blow air into us . . . we can feel a little bit of air going into us . . . we start to get a little bigger . . . there is more air going into us . . . we are getting bigger and bigger . . . we have to stand up now . . . bigger and bigger . . . when there is too much air in us, we will all have to scream when we pop . . . we are getting so big that we can't stand it anymore . . . bigger and bigger . . . get ready . . . everyone . . . "POP"!!

EXERCISE 4

From Eggs to Candles

The floor is covered with millions of eggs . . . we have always wanted to walk on eggs . . . we are wearing giant shoes, and we can break 50 eggs at a time . . . we stomp around until we have broken all of the eggs . . . let's make sure that all of the eggs are broken . . . get every egg.

We are now nice big FUZZY SPIDERS . . . we are trying to crawl through all the egg "goo" on the floor . . . we all have eight legs, and we have "goo" on every one of our feet . . . we have so far to go, and it is so hard to move all these legs with the "goo" on them . . . we finally reach our destination, and we stop for a rest.

We have all become RAG DOLLS, and we are trying to stand up . . . we want to stand up and see what it feels like . . . we are so floppy, and our arms and legs are so loose . . . we try to stand up, but we can't.

We are all FEATHERS on the ground . . . a very small breeze comes along and makes us move a little . . . it is a gentle breeze, and it feels good . . . the breeze starts to get a little stronger . . . we are getting carried through the air now . . . it is getting stronger and stronger . . . we have each become the center of a TORNADO . . . it is one of the biggest and strongest tornadoes that ever was . . . we are twisting and turning . . . turning . . . the storm has reached its peak . . . and it is starting to calm down now . . . it has become a very gentle breeze again . . . we have been left standing very still with our arms down to our sides . . . we are standing very very still.

We have all become CANDLES. There is a flame burning on the top of every one of us . . . it feels very relaxing . . . the wax is starting to drip down our sides . . . we are starting to get shorter . . . we are getting very short . . . the wax keeps on dripping . . . we are all very short now . . . it feels very good . . . we are now only a pool of wax . . . a very relaxed pool of wax.

starts to slide slowly out of the jar . . . we have all become a mass of stickiness . . . we all move slowly and go in any direction we want . . . we are all very slow and sticky.

We have all become PEOPLE . . . we are standing up and walking in a shallow stream . . . we are trying to cross to the other side . . . it is getting deeper, and we are using smooth stones in the creek to help us get across . . . we have to jump from stone to stone . . . some of the stones are very slippery, and sometimes we fall . . . we keep on trying . . . and we all get to the other side . . . when we get to the other side, we all find shoes with LARGE SPRINGS on the bottoms of them . . . we put the shoes on our feet . . . every step we take makes us jump . . . we can't stand still . . . we just keep jumping and jumping . . . we jump higher and higher . . . we have jumped so much that we can't jump anymore.

We all fall down on the grass and relax. We close our eyes and listen to the sound of the creek and to the birds . . . it feels so good . . . suddenly we all open our eyes . . . we have all lost our voices and we can't make a sound . . . we all see a BIG BLACK BEAR coming toward us. We are so scared that we can't move. We try to scream, but we can't . . . we try to move, but we can't . . . the bear is getting closer . . . he is only ten feet away from us now . . . we want to scream . . . when he gets three feet away from us, we will scream as loud as we can . . . he is getting closer and closer . . . we want to scream . . . he is four feet away . . . we can't move . . . he is three feet away . . . SCREAM!!

Note: After conducting these exercises a few times, you'll become familiar with the types of imagery that the group enjoys most. You can then adapt these passages and create exciting new ideas along the lines suggested here.

EXERCISE 5

From Honey to a Scream

Let's all get close together. We are HONEY IN A JAR. The jar tips over, and the honey

Pantomime

The following exercises offer a variety of pantomime and guessing games that, while fun to do, also help children become less inhibited and more specific with their actions. When a student needs to be more specific, the instructor should "side coach"—that is, make suggestions and ask questions (e.g., "think of how you can make it more believable," "try to keep your actions smaller," "try to move around less," "what does it feel like?") while carefully watching the student's work. It is very important to let the performer know that his or her work is being understood and appreciated.

Often, very strong characters emerge from pantomime exercises. In such instances, the teacher can easily give the character or characters improvisational situations which allow the actors to work with the new character(s).

When conducting a pantomime "guessing game," allow each student to finish his or her work completely before encouraging the class to guess what the student is portraying.

EXERCISE 6
One Object Show

Select one of the following objects (or something similarly simple and nondescript), and place it before the class: small square tablecloth, long piece of string, small piece of driftwood, small flat board, large white handkerchief, cardboard box, broom handle, brown paper bag, long flat stick, block of wood, big hunk of cotton, empty jar, or a small empty box.

Tell the students to think of what each might "do" with the article in front of the class so as to portray what the object means to them *without saying anything* to the other students. The object of the exercise is for the class to guess what the article "becomes" to each performer.

Encourage the students to keep their

pantomime short and simple, and remind the rest of the class to allow each person to finish performing before starting to guess.

Note: Keeping the objects simple encourages the students to use their imaginations; avoid including objects that strongly suggest what they "should" be to the performers.

EXERCISE 7
Passing Exercise

Everyone, including the leader, stands in a circle. Explain that all of them will be "passing" imaginary objects from one person to another. Among these imaginary objects might be a basketball, a balloon, an ice cube,

From *Creative Dramatics for Children* by Maureen McCurry Cresci © 1989 Scott, Foresman and Company.

paper with honey on it, a feather, a three-pound weight, a snake, a giant bubble, a big dog, a bowl of soup, a diamond, and an egg.

Although the leader tells the students what the object is, he or she *does not* give examples of how to act. The key here is for each student to decide how the object "feels" to him or her. After saying what the object is, however, the leader should continue asking the children questions: "How big is it?" "Is it heavy or light?" "What does it feel like?" and so forth.

EXERCISE 8

Basic Business

This exercise, though not conducted as a guessing game, is an excellent introduction to pantomime. Start by suggesting a piece of "business" for a student to do in front of the class. Because the class is aware of what each student is trying to portray, it can learn a great deal by watching and offering suggestions to each performer.

Encourage the students to think carefully about any tools or special equipment they would use in doing this business. Where would such equipment be kept? How big is it? What does it feel like? Side coach by making helpful suggestions while a student is doing the exercise. Typically, beginning students leave objects "hanging in the air" and forget where they have "left" things.

After each student completes the exercise, discuss whether or not the performance was convincing. Ask the class for suggestions about what the student might have done differently.

Here are some suggestions for student portrayals:

1. Carry a very heavy pail of water across the room. Then pour the water out, and carry the empty pail back.

2. Open a carton of milk. Pour the milk into a glass, and drink the milk.
3. Put toothpaste on your toothbrush, and brush your teeth.
4. Cut a piece of cake. Then eat several bites of it without using a fork.
5. Play a game of "jacks."
6. Open a book. Read a few lines. Then tear a page out of the book, fold it up, and put it in your pocket. Put the book down.
7. Open a package of gum and take out a piece. Remove the wrapper from the piece, and then put the gum in your mouth and chew it.
8. Carry a vase and a pair of scissors out into the garden. Use the scissors to cut a single rose. Put the rose into the vase.
9. Open a bottle of mouthwash, and pour a little into a glass. Put some of the mouthwash in your mouth, swish it around, and then spit it out.
10. Start to write your name on the blackboard, but when you are halfway finished, the chalk breaks. Pick up one of the pieces of chalk and start over.
11. Take off your pullover sweater, place it on the floor, and fold it. Lie down on the floor, and put your head on the folded sweater.
12. Put flea powder on your very large and very angry cat.
13. Make a peanut butter and jelly sandwich. Eat a few bites.
14. Thread a needle, and tie a knot in the thread.
15. Blow up a balloon, and tie a knot in the end of it. Bounce the balloon up in the air.
16. Bring paint supplies into a room. Paint a section of a wall.
17. Open a soft drink can, and drink from the can.
18. Break three eggs into a bowl. Beat the eggs with a fork.
19. Hammer a nail into a wall, and hang a heavy picture from the nail.
20. Use a can opener to open a can of beans. Spoon the beans out of the can into a pan.

21. Sew two pieces of fabric together with a needle and thread.
22. Gather all the materials, and start to build a brick wall.
23. Open an envelope and read the letter inside.
24. Brush your teeth, and comb your hair.
25. Try several times to make a phone call, but the line is always busy.
26. Give a bath to a very large and very energetic dog.
27. Pick some spilled beads off the floor, and put them into a small box.
28. Wash your hands with a very small piece of soap.
29. Cut out a string of paper dolls.

EXERCISE 9

Imaginary Object from Hat

This exercise begins with each student drawing the name of an object from a hat or box and telling the instructor what he or she has drawn. When using this exercise with pre-school children, draw simple pictures of the objects on slips of paper instead of writing the objects' names.

The student may either "use" the object through pantomime or "become" the object. The instructor, who knows what object the student drew, can side coach throughout the performance. When the performer finishes, the rest of the class tries to guess what the student was "using" or had "become." This is a very enjoyable—often very funny—exercise that children love doing over and over.

Among the imaginary objects you might consider putting in the hat are a flower, a typewriter, a football, a guitar, a sewing machine, an octopus, a mouse, a fencing foil, a telephone, a snake, a piece of bubblegum, a rope, ballet slippers, cowboy boots, a bicycle, a yo-yo, an egg beater, a ball, a rubber band, a tire, a mosquito, a boat, a bottle of ketchup, a horse, a cat, boxing gloves, a giant spring, a hammer, a crab, a bloodhound dog, a teapot, a shovel, a thumbtack, a paintbrush, a lemon, a balloon, a chicken, an egg, a bird, scissors, a fish, an axe, an electric fan, a monster, and a bull fighter.

EXERCISE 10

Imaginary Object—Two People

This exercise, which is not worked as a guessing game, involves students working in pairs. The instructor gives each pair of students an activity to perform and a very short rehearsal—with side coaching, if necessary—before the pair performs the activity in front of the group. Among the activities you might suggest are folding a blanket, pulling taffy, playing on a teeter-totter, playing catch, playing tennis, playing tug-of-war with a rope, playing ping-pong, and playing jump rope.

After the performance, ask the class for helpful suggestions. Then have the student pair repeat the activity performance, incorporating the suggestions from the class.

EXERCISE 11

Come into a Room for a Purpose

Conducted as a guessing game, this exercise is designed to make one action compelling and to help the student follow through with one "clean" and uncomplicated destination.

Start by asking the students to think of one room in their homes that they would go into for one particular action. Then have each student perform by going into the "room," doing the action, and leaving. Each performance should be very short and kept very simple from beginning to end.

The class is to guess what room the person went into and what action the person did there. The exercise can be expanded by asking the class for suggestions on how the performance might be improved and then having the student repeat the performance using the class's suggestions.

EXERCISE 12
Become the Toys

Discuss different kinds of toys and recreational equipment. Ask the children to name their favorite toys and sports. Ask them what they would be if they could "become" a toy or piece of recreational equipment. How would they act?

When each child has selected a favorite toy or piece of sports equipment, have the whole class "become" these objects together. Then, during the exercise, continue asking for suggestions. The children will come up with more ideas while they are performing the exercise.

Here are some suggestions to get things started: a superball, pogo stick, tin soldiers, a jack-in-the-box, a slinky, a spinning top, an airplane, etc.

EXERCISE 13
How Do I Help at Home?

Have the students get up one at a time and SHOW the group—through the actions they use—how they help at home. It is very important to let each student finish before anyone in the class starts guessing.

If the group cannot figure out what the performer is doing, then have the person reveal what the action is. Ask the class for suggestions on how the action could be performed in a more understandable way. Have the performer repeat the action, using the class's suggestions.

EXERCISE 14
What Am I Carrying?

Ask each student to "carry" something across the room in front of the class. Although you should encourage the children to think of their own objects, you might suggest as examples such things as a bird, balloon, feather, person, book, snowball, piano, butterfly, and diamond.

The group tries to guess what is being carried by how the child handles it. For this reason, tell the students that their objects cannot be kept inside of a box.

EXERCISE 15
What Am I Doing?

This exercise is not conducted as a guessing game. Give each student a suggestion of something to do—e.g., bake a cake, get dressed, do homework, feed a puppy, spread butter on a piece of bread, put on and tie shoes, dry off after a swim, plant a row of seeds in a garden.

Tell the students to think of the supplies they will need and how they will go about performing the activity in front of the class.

Give them all a few minutes to prepare. Then, during the performances, side coach when necessary. Following each performance, ask the class for suggestions as to how the action might be portrayed more clearly.

EXERCISE 16

What Am I Eating?

This exercise is not a guessing game. Give each student a suggestion for something to "eat." Possible suggestions include a piece of pizza, a slice of watermelon, a hot dog, an apple, spaghetti, a bunch of grapes, fried chicken, a carrot, an ice cream cone, a banana, a hamburger, and a grapefruit.

Tell the students to think about how they will touch the food, hold it, and use their mouth when "eating" it. Help by making suggestions while each student is performing in front of the group.

EXERCISE 17

What Is My Occupation?

Conduct this exercise as a guessing game. Start by giving each student an occupation, explaining the kinds of tasks involved, how the person would dress and move, the types of tools that would be used, etc. Then give the performer a few moments to concentrate before getting up in front of the class. Here are some examples of occupations for this exercise: hair stylist, dentist, dog groomer, pianist, gardener, dancer, bricklayer, carpenter, lumberjack, manicurist, wrestler, lion tamer, and opera singer.

EXERCISE 18

What Animal in the Zoo Am I?

Have a discussion about favorite animals in the zoo. Then ask each child to portray his or her favorite animal for the rest of the class. Younger children enjoy becoming the same animals in a group.

EXERCISE 19

The Veterinarian's Office

To start this exercise, which is a guessing game, tell the students that you want them to think of a pet that they would like to own. Explain that they will be taking the pet to visit a veterinarian who is capable of caring for any type of animal in the world.

Have each student take his or her pet into the veterinarian's office. In so doing, the student should show the group—by the way he or she handles the pet, carries it, leads it, talks to it (without revealing what it is), puts it down, and responds to its actions—just what species it is.

If the class cannot guess what type of animal it is, then the student must "become" the animal, thereby making for easier identification.

EXERCISE 20

The Foreigner in an American Store

In this exercise, each student pretends to be a foreigner visiting the United States. The "foreigner" goes into a store and wants to

From *Creative Dramatics for Children* by Maureen McCurry Cresci © 1989 Scott, Foresman and Company.

buy three items. Another student, the only one in the class who is not told what the three items are, plays the storekeeper.

The storekeeper can ask questions, but the "foreigner" must request the items and respond to the storekeeper's questions only by gesturing in pantomime. The "visiting" student tries to get the storekeeper to understand what he or she wants to buy.

This exercise gives everyone a chance to "be in on the secret." If possible, give every student a turn at being the storekeeper.

EXERCISE 21

Costume Exercise

Start this exercise, conducted as a guessing game, by giving all the students identical materials with which to make costumes. These materials may include an old white sheet cut up into large squares, colored paper, butcher paper, crayons, yarn, string, feathers, glue, sequins, scissors, and tape.

Encourage the children to be selective in choosing their costume materials. Tell them to think of an animal, toy, or other object that they would like to make themselves look like. When they complete their costumes, have the students go to the front of the class and portray their chosen animal or object by acting like it and making noises like it in addition to looking like it through use of the costume. See if the class can recognize what the performer is trying to be.

EXERCISE 22

Become a Musical Instrument

Conduct this exercise as a guessing game. Tell the students that they are to "become"

musical instruments. Although you can suggest such instruments as a piano, accordion, harp, tambourine, guitar, bagpipes, drum, harmonica, and flute, encourage the students to come up with their own ideas.

When each child has chosen an instrument, he or she should portray it through using flexible body motions and making appropriate sounds. The rest of the class tries to guess each student's instrument.

EXERCISE 23

Become a Mechanical Object

Start this exercise, which is conducted as a guessing game, by having the students draw slips of paper. On each slip have the name of an object to portray—e.g., a lawn mower, record player, blender, power saw, clock, bicycle, car, jet plane, television set, sewing machine, vacuum cleaner, power drill, washing machine, radio, egg beater, toaster, and an electric fan.

Each student is to "become" the moving mechanical device, including the appropriate mechanical sounds. The instructor should be aware of what each student is portraying in order to supply side coaching as necessary. The rest of class tries to guess what mechanical object each student is portraying.

EXERCISE 24

Become the Emotion

This exercise is not to be conducted as a guessing game.

Phase 1. Discuss a variety of emotions with the class: love, fear, anger, jealousy, happiness, sadness, greed, hate, pity, gloom, hysteria, shyness, fright, meanness, ecstasy. Then have each student select an emotion he or she can portray. Point out that emotions can be portrayed at various degrees and intensities, and encourage the students to add sounds as appropriate. Emphasize, however, that the purpose of the exercise is to become the emotion itself, not a person experiencing the emotion.

Phase 2. Tell the students to think about two characters: Miss Pity and Mr. Gloom. Ask what kind of people these characters would be. Give the students specific situations to act out individually, using one of these characters. (*See* "Actions for Solo Characters" in Part 4.)

Phase 3. Put several of the students in a situation together, and have them use characters from Phase 1. Funny combinations would result from combining "Miss Fright," "Mr. Anger," and "Mr. Love." (*See* "Actions for Characters in a Group" in Part 4.)

EXERCISE 25
Become the Element

You conduct this exercise exactly the same way as 24, except that you substitute natural elements—wind, rain, fire, lightning, thunder, and earthquake—for human emotions. Be sure to include characters acting in solo situations and characters acting in group situations.

EXERCISE 26
Become a Color

Conduct this exercise in exactly the same manner as 24 and 25, substituting colors for emotions and elements. Be sure to conclude with characters acting in group situations.

Note: After students develop strong characters in exercises 24, 25, and 26, the exercises can easily be carried into improvisational situations. Appropriate improvisational situations for one or more of the characters can be found in Part 4.

Spontaneous Emotional Response

EXERCISE 27
Temper Tantrum

This exercise is a very effective release, and once children have done it, they want to continue doing it. By providing a means of letting children have a controlled temper tantrum, the exercise releases a lot of inhibitions and even assists in calming a group down. It's especially appropriate to use when the children have a great deal of energy.

Two students work together. One child wants something, and the other will not give it. The child is to get angrier and angrier, fall on the floor, and kick and scream—all without touching the other child. The child continues having the tantrum until tiring of the exercise.

EXERCISE 28

The Big Scream

This is an excellent exercise to conduct at the end of class. Have the children sit or lie down. Tell them all to think of something that would be very scary if it were to happen to them.

Now tell them that whatever scary thing they imagined is starting to happen to them and that every minute it is getting worse and becoming more frightening. Tell them that they want to scream—they actually can feel a big scream inside of them—but their screams "can't get out."

Continue building this scenario until the children are all very rigid and want to scream. Then, on the count of five, let them scream.

EXERCISE 29

The Big Laugh

Another excellent exercise to conduct at the end of class, this one starts by telling the children to either sit or lie down and think of something that is very funny. Tell them that though they want to laugh at it, they can't seem to make a noise.

Build this up until the children act as though they are about to explode. Then tell them that they have suddenly regained their

voices and can laugh as hard as they want.

An alternative method of conducting this exercise involves telling the children that you are going to walk around the room with a big bunch of feathers and tickle all of them. Then walk around the room and softly touch each child.

EXERCISE 30

The Giant Spring

This is an effective exercise to conduct at the end of class. Start by telling the class: "You are all giant springs in separate boxes. I have a magic key that will wind you up as tight as you can go. I am going to wind you all up so tight that you are squeezed inside your boxes."

Then go around the room with your imaginary key, winding up each child. Continue by saying: "I am going to keep winding you tighter and tighter. The only thing that can help you is when I clap my hands together. That will open all the boxes. What happens to springs when they suddenly are let out of boxes? I am winding you tighter and tighter. Get ready."

Clap hands.

EXERCISE 31

Laugh

Have a few students take turns sitting in front of an imaginary television set. Tell them that they are going to "watch" something very funny. Encourage them, when they are ready, to laugh hard and in different ways so that the laughter seems convincing to the rest of the class watching them.

Note: When working with students under eight years old, give them a small empty box to look into. Have them pretend that when they peek into the box they see something very funny inside it.

EXERCISE 32

Cry

You conduct this exercise exactly as you did 31, except that you have the students respond by crying at something sad they see on the imaginary television set.

EXERCISE 33

Get Mad—Cry—Laugh (By Yourself)

Tell the students to pretend that they are watching television or a ball game. While watching, they are to experience something that makes them angry, something that makes them sad, and something that makes them burst into laughter. Encourage them to use their emotions to think of situations that would change their moods so drastically. Give each student plenty of time to prepare to act in a believable way.

EXERCISE 34

Tantrum—Cry—Laugh (With a Partner)

This exercise is conducted in pairs. Tell the students to keep it very simple and to take plenty of time. The idea is for the person expressing the emotions to pay careful attention to what the other person is saying before starting to react.

The exercise consists of one partner telling the other something that will motivate him or her to have a furious "tantrum," followed by something else that will make the partner "cry," and finally something that will make him or her "laugh." When they finish the exercise, have the partners switch parts.

EXERCISE 35

Act Out an Emotion on Different Levels

This exercise can help children become aware of how emotions can be experienced on different levels. There is a good deal of difference, for example, between being slightly angry and very angry.

When working with children who are eight years and younger, have them stand in a circle and pretend as though they are "passing around" the emotion. Start by telling one child what the emotion is and the degree of it—e.g., "I am giving you . . . *very, very excited.*" The child is to show the suggested level of emotion and then pass it on to the next child in the circle. Older children (9-12 years old) also stand in a circle, but they can all do the exercise together instead of "passing around" the emotion. In this case, the leader merely suggests the emotion and the level of intensity for the group.

More advanced students can get up in front of the class as individuals and show each suggested level of emotion by themselves.

Besides slightly angry/very angry and a little excited/very excited, other emotions and levels include a little happy/very happy, a little sad/very sad, a little surprised/very surprised, a little greedy/very greedy, and slightly terrified/extremely terrified.

Relaxation Exercises

The exercises in this group are well suited for use at the beginning of class or after a very energetic activity.

EXERCISE 36
The Ocean

Have the children sit or lie down with their eyes closed, and slowly read the following passage to them:

Think only of your breathing . . . breathe very slowly and very deeply . . . make your inhales and exhales the same length . . . think only of your breathing . . . imagine the ocean by your side . . . you are lying on the sand . . . you can see the waves . . . when you inhale, the waves come to you . . . when you exhale, the waves go out. Each time that the waves go out, your nervous energy goes with the ocean . . . let the ocean take your tension away . . . inhale, bring the ocean to you . . . exhale . . . let your tensions go. All of your tensions are now at sea . . . let each wave that comes to you bring you peace . . . tranquility . . . let the ocean take away your cares . . . let it bring you peace.

EXERCISE 37
A Meadow

Have the children sit or lie down with their eyes closed, and slowly read the following passage to them:

You are in a meadow . . . the grass is tall and green and the wind is softly blowing . . . think only of how very pretty everything is . . . You can hear a little creek close by . . . there are lots of birds overhead . . . all you can hear are the birds and the noises of the creek . . . and you can feel the soft wind . . . listen to the water . . . to the sounds of the birds . . . just relax.

EXERCISE 38
A Golden Light

Have the children sit or lie down with their eyes closed, and slowly read the following passage to them:

Everyone relax and be very still . . . your eyes are all closed . . . everything is totally black . . . close everything out of your minds except the blackness . . . just look at the soft gentle blackness . . . far away in the middle there is a small white light . . . just relax and look at it . . . the light is slowly getting larger . . . it is a sort of golden glow . . . as it gets closer it feels warm and very good . . . the warmth from it makes you completely relax . . . it is getting larger . . . there is very little black now on the outside . . . the golden light is making you limp and very peaceful . . . there is now only the golden light in front of your eyes . . . it makes you feel totally calm . . . very refreshed . . . relaxed . . . .

EXERCISE 39

Ideas for Relaxation

Here are some suggestions to make to the children during relaxation periods. Have them concentrate on the suggestion until they feel relaxed.

1. A candle is lit and gradually burns down into a pool of wax.
2. A feather floats gently to the ground.
3. You are on a raft in the middle of a peaceful pond.
4. We are listening to a soft wind and gentle rain.

If the children seem a little sleepy after the relaxation period, tell them to jump up and down and shake themselves out.

Sensitivity Exercises

These are quiet exercises that can help children become aware of and able to discuss with others how they feel about the events and circumstances going on around them. Sensitivity exercises are very effective following a relaxation exercise.

EXERCISE 40

What Do You Hear?

Have the children sit on the floor in a scattered group. Tell them to close their eyes and to forget about everything except their ears and what their ears can hear. Tell them that they are going to be put in different imaginary places and that they should concentrate only on what they can "hear" in each new place.
    Here are some examples to give the children:

1. You are at the beach. There are lots of people around.
2. You are at a carnival.
3. You are at an airport.
4. You are in a children's playground.
5. You are in a supermarket.
6. You are in a forest.
7. You are in your own back yard.

Instruct the children to raise their hands when they "hear" something and then to share what they heard with the group.

EXERCISE 41

What Do You See?

Conduct this exercise exactly the same as 40, with the children sitting on the floor in a scattered group with their eyes closed, but this time tell them to forget everything except for their eyes and what their eyes can see. Tell them to concentrate on what they can "see" in each imaginary place.

Here are some examples to give the children:

1. You are waiting for a bus.
2. You are sitting on a crowded bus.
3. You are watching a parade go by.
4. You are looking out of your favorite window.
5. You are walking on the sand at a beach.
6. You are in a children's playground.

Instruct the children to raise their hands when they "see" something and then to share what they saw with the group.

EXERCISE 42

What Do You Smell?

Conduct this exercise exactly the same as 40 and 41, with the children sitting on the floor in a scattered group with their eyes closed, but this time tell them to forget everything except for their noses and what their noses can smell. Tell them to concentrate on what they can "smell" in each imaginary place.

Here are some examples to give the children:

1. You are at the grocery store.
2. You are in the park.
3. You are waiting in the doctor's office.
4. You are camping overnight.
5. You are standing at a hot dog stand.
6. You are in the rain.
7. You are in a car that is stopped in heavy traffic.
8. You are sitting on a crowded bus.
9. You are in your kitchen.

Instruct the children to raise their hands when they "smell" something and then to share what they smelled with the group.

EXERCISE 43

Feel Imaginary Objects

Have the children sit in a circle with their eyes closed. Have them hold out their hands, and tell them that they are going to be handed imaginary objects. Each child is to "feel" the object and describe to the class what it "feels" like before passing the object along to the next student.

Here are some examples of imaginary objects to suggest to the children:

1. a baby bird
2. a porcupine
3. ice cubes
4. thumbtacks
5. a piece of velvet
6. a little snake
7. whipped cream
8. rose petals
9. an apple
10. an elf (2" tall)
11. lots of little marshmallows
12. a basketball
13. a puppy
14. mud
15. a ping-pong ball
16. sand
17. glue

As the children pass the imaginary object along, ask them: "What does it feel like?" "Is it moving?" "Is it light or heavy?"

EXERCISE 44

Feeling Things Blindfolded

This exercise is especially fun to do around Halloween. Start by having the children sit blindfolded in a circle, and give each one a towel. Then hand one of the following real objects to each student:

1. pieces of a gelatin dessert
2. a bag full of wet marshmallows
3. several peeled grapes
4. wet oatmeal
5. several strands of hemp (rope)
6. a long piece of gauze
7. broken eggs in a container
8. a natural sponge
9. marbles in a small plastic bag
10. a large wad of thread
11. sliced peaches in an open container
12. wet clay

Tell the children that they should concentrate on describing what their object feels like rather than try to guess what it is. Then, after they have discussed the objects, have them take off their blindfolds. Allow them to talk freely about how the various things made them feel.

EXERCISE 45

Hearing and Smelling Things—Blindfolded

Bring to class a number of items that have a distinctive smell and other items that make interesting sounds. Among the "smell" objects you might consider are spices, newspaper, oil paint, wood, mud, leather, a flower, straw, bath powder, and soap. Items that make interesting sounds include wind chimes, a pitch pipe, a paper punch used on light cardboard, aluminum foil being torn slowly, a wooden hammer tapping a block of wood, rice poured into a tin cup, a ping-pong ball bounced once, a fingernail run over sandpaper, a stapler used on heavy paper, cellophane being crumpled, and one beat on a small drum.

Have the students sit in a circle. Blindfold one student at a time. Give each blindfolded student something to sniff, and then talk about how the item makes him or her feel and what meaning the item might have for the student. Make clear that the student is not to try to guess what the item is but rather just talk about his or her reactions to the item. Repeat the procedure with the items that make interesting sounds.

Extending the Activities to other Areas of the Curriculum

WRITING

In exercises 1 through 5 and 22 through 25, the children imagine that they are many

different things. In poetry, something that is compared to or described as another thing is called a metaphor. Have your students write a poem that includes some simple metaphors. Start by having them choose ten things that they could imagine themselves being. Then have them write a ten-line poem, with each line beginning, "I am . . . ."

Example:
I am a tree,
I am the wind,
I am a rock . . .

After doing Exercise 5, have the children talk about how it felt to imagine the bear getting closer and closer and not being able to scream. Then have the children write about and illustrate a scary dream they once had or a real event that made them very frightened.

Check out a collection of scary stories from the library, or have the children tell some ghost stories that they know. Discuss how the author or story teller builds suspense in the stories. Then have your students write their own original scary tales.

After Exercise 23, have each student pick a mechanical object and write a story from the point of view of that object. For example, someone could write about "A Day in the Life of an Egg Beater" as told from the egg beater's perspective.

Use Exercise 44 to stimulate descriptive writing. Have the students pick one of the objects used in the exercise, and then challenge them to describe every line, every curve in a paragraph or two. Tell them to imagine that they must describe their object to a blind person.

ART

In exercises 1 through 5 and 22 through 25, the students imagine themselves becoming different things. Have each student pick something and draw him- or herself as that thing (e.g., Samantha as a bottle of ketchup, Michael as the wind). This art project may be done in conjunction with the metaphor-writing exercise (*see above*) or by itself.

After doing Exercise 24, see if your students can illustrate Miss Pity or Mr. Gloom, etc. as cartoon characters. Then have them work together in groups to merge their characters into comic strips with dialogue for their characters.

Exercises 27 through 35 can stimulate some "mood" art projects. Ask your students to create a picture that conveys a particular emotion. Let them experiment with different colors to see how color can change the mood of a picture. Bring in some books of art prints from the library—or visit an art museum—to observe how great artists use color to convey emotion in their work.

The same exercises can give rise to some experimentation with sculpture. Have your students create a soft sculpture out of clay, fabric, papier mache, wood, or other available materials. The sculpture should convey the emotion of their choice and be named appropriately: e.g., Greed, Love, Pity, Happiness, Jealousy, etc.

After doing Exercise 35, the children can work in pairs to sketch various degrees of emotion. First one partner uses facial expressions to convey a low level of the chosen emotion; the other partner sketches the details of these facial expressions. Then the first partner greatly intensifies the level of emotion, challenging his or her partner to sketch the detail of the change in another drawing next to the first one. The pair may then switch roles and choose another emotion.

SOCIAL STUDIES

The student performing a pantomime in Exercise 9 could choose an object associated with a career—e.g., a stethoscope or a hammer. After the class guesses the object, challenge the students to list all the professions in which the object would play a significant role.

When doing Exercise 17, have the students pantomime an occupation that interests them. You might even have them follow up with an oral or written report about that career.

Upon completing Exercise 20, ask the "foreigners" how they felt trying to make themselves understood while unable to communicate in English. Have your students find out when and from where their ancestors came to America, and ask them to share some family stories about early experiences in this country.

Exercise 27 could open up a discussion about power and how people manipulate each other. Start by talking about what happened in the exercise, and then move on to how we manipulate parents or friends. Then see if students can relate this discussion to political parties, elected leaders, or even nations.

After the blindfold exercises 44 and 45, have a discussion about what life is like for someone who is blind, deaf, or has some other physical handicap. This could lead into a unit on disabled people and the current issues relevant to them.

SCIENCE

After Exercise 16, discuss with your students which of the imaginary foods eaten were the healthiest—and why. Also discuss why the other foods were not as healthy (in terms of cholesterol, sugar, etc.).

After doing Exercise 23, bring in some real mechanical objects or appliances for the students to take apart and explore how they work. Get some books or a film on simple machines, and have your students create their own simple machines, using easily accessible materials.

Exercises 40 through 45 could be used in conjunction with a unit on the five senses. These exercises could also stimulate study on exactly how each of the senses works.

PART **2**
LEARNING CONTROL

The exercises in this section are designed to develop concentration and discipline. While Part 1 focused on loosening up and letting creativity flow, Part 2 focuses on mastering techniques that help shape that creative energy into art. Some of the exercises teach physical control and some teach mental control, but all of them require students to stay within prescribed guidelines and follow specific directions to sharpen their acting skills.

In addition to teaching physical control and mental control, some of the exercises in this section are designed to motivate children to develop concentration and discipline. These exercises utilize a contest format in which the children can compete against one another in a variety of "who can do something the longest" activities.

Introducing the Exercises to Your Students

Ask the children, "Do you think that dancers, painters, or writers can produce good work by just being creative and talented? Do creative and talented people also have to practice techniques? How do they balance creativity and discipline?"

Have the students come up with examples from their own lives. Most of them will be able to relate the balance of creativity and discipline in their own writing. First they let ideas flow, but then they use techniques of effective writing to shape their work into a presentable form. Explain that this next phase of drama exercises involves learning the concentration and control necessary to good acting.

From *Creative Dramatics for Children* by Maureen McCurry Cresci © 1989 Scott, Foresman and Company.

Physical Control

The exercises in this section are concerned with helping students concentrate on and follow through with simple physical actions.

EXERCISE 46
Fall Down

It is important to teach children how to fall down properly without hurting themselves. The technique involves three basic steps:

1. Fall gently to knees.
2. Swing hips to one side. Sit down on the side of the hips.
3. Slide the corresponding arm straight out and fall to the side, ending up with the head resting on the arm.

After the students have gone through these steps a few times slowly, have the class pick up speed until they all can fall down in one smooth movement.

EXERCISE 47
Laugh at Your Partner

The object of this exercise, which is done in pairs, is for one child to laugh at the other. The child being laughed at tries to carry on a very serious conversation, but everything he or she says is regarded as very funny by the other child.

Tell the students to try to be as convincing as possible in their given assignments. The "serious" child is to continue talking in a sincere manner while the "laughing" partner is to try to find actual humor in what he or she is hearing. Then let them switch parts. Give each child a simple topic to talk about.

EXERCISE 48
Do Something Two Ways

Have each student act out a different situation as it would be handled by two very different kinds of people who realistically might be put in the situation. The children act out one character at a time.

Here are examples of situations and characters:

Situation: Giving a dog a bath
Characters: 1. A professional dog groomer
2. A person who is afraid of dogs

Situation: Selling all-occasion cards door-to-door
Characters: 1. A very shy person
2. A professional salesperson

Situation: Brushing teeth in front of a mirror
Characters: 1. A three-year-old child
2. A person with false teeth

Situation: Walking your dog in the park
Characters: 1. A person who weighs much
less than the dog
2. A very old person

Situation: Getting splashed with mud from a
car while crossing the street
Characters: 1. A person carrying a lot of
packages
2. A person wearing new clothes

Situation: Exercising in front of a mirror
Characters: 1. A person who loves to
exercise
2. A person who needs to lose
200 pounds

Situation: Watching television
Characters: 1. A small child watching a
cartoon
2. An adult watching a soap
opera

Situation: Trying to swat a fly with a fly
swatter
Characters: 1. A person who doesn't see
very well
2. A professional tennis player

EXERCISE 49
Walking Different Ways

Have the students spread out so that they
can work without watching one another.
Give each student a different walking
situation—e.g., walking barefoot in a field of
clover, walking in cold water, walking
through feathers, walking through ice cubes,
walking on sharp rocks, walking on logs in a
stream, walking through deep and very hot
desert sand, walking barefoot in mud,
walking on the bottom of the sea with very
heavy shoes, walking through heavy rain,
walking through spider webs.

Students work in their own areas, trying to
walk in ways appropriate to their situations.

EXERCISE 50
Action in Three Speeds

Give each student a simple action to perform
in front of the class. Examples of such
actions include pitching a baseball, twirling a
baton, brushing hair, threading a needle,
putting on a hat and coat, sitting down and
tying shoes, digging with a shovel, shooting
an arrow, rolling a bowling ball, taking a
shower, hitting a golf ball with a club,
hitting a tennis ball with a racquet, putting
on socks, and throwing a dart.

Tell the students to do their actions three
times at three different speeds: First, do the
action in the normal way; second, do the
action in slow-motion; and third, do the
action in a speeded-up motion.

EXERCISE 51
Improvisation With "Marks"

In film and theatre productions, marks on
the floor or stage are commonly used to give
the actor a point to move towards. Within a
single scene, an actor may have several
different marks to which he or she moves
and stands upon while working. The purpose
of this exercise is to acquaint young actors
and actresses with this technique.

Put two marks on the floor (red or white
tape works very well). Divide the class into
pairs, and have each pair think of a situation
in which one person would walk into a room
(and stand on a mark) and call the other
person into the room (who would stand on
the other mark). The object of the exercise
is to learn how to use the marks *without
looking down at them.*

Although the situations should be kept
very simple, students who master the
technique may move on to somewhat more
complicated scenes involving four marks
(two marks each).

EXERCISE 52

The Mirror

Phase 1. Divide the class into pairs, and designate one partner in each pair as A and the other as B. Have the A's and B's face each other and pretend that their partners are their image in a mirror. Tell the A's what part of the body to move. Begin with simple movements, and instruct the students to move very slowly so that their mirror image can follow.

For example, tell the A's to raise their left arms very slowly in front of them and then very slowly back to their sides. The B's should duplicate these movements exactly. Then have the B's initiate a simple action for the A's to follow. Here are some suggestions of simple actions to use for this exercise:

Raise your arm in front of you, make a fist, relax your hand, and put your arm back down.

Raise one foot about five inches off the floor, point your toes towards the ground, and then put your foot back down.

Move both arms in front of you. Clasp your hands, relax your hands, and then put your arms back down.

Pretend that you are walking, but stay in the same place. Raise one foot slowly, put it down, and then repeat with the other foot.

Phase 2. Again, have the students work in pairs. Tell them to sit down and face each other. Give them suggestions for facial expressions to portray—e.g., worry, surprise, happiness, fright, meanness, satisfaction, greed, pity, sadness, pain. Remind them to work very slowly so that their partners can follow. Give each partner a turn at initiating a facial expression.

Phase 3. In this phase of the exercise, students have an opportunity to follow through with a complete action. Again, have them work in pairs, acting as the mirror image of their partner's movements.

Possible actions for this exercise include

From *Creative Dramatics for Children* by Maureen McCurry Cresci © 1989 Scott, Foresman and Company.

buttoning up a shirt, putting suntan lotion on your arms, scratching yourself in different places, washing your face with soap and a wash cloth, wiping a dirty spot off your face, combing hair, and putting lotion on your face.

Using Control to Win a Contest

The exercises in this group are designed to help children forget themselves by motivating them to become competitive with each other. For most children, being singled out as "the winner" is very special and an ample enough reward for their efforts.

EXERCISE 53

Who Can Do Things the Longest?

Have the students do the same action individually, competing against each other to see who can do the action the longest. Good ideas for this contest include laughing the longest, crying the longest, staying angry the longest (while the class laughs), talking to the class the longest, asking the most questions of the class, and answering the most questions from the class.

EXERCISE 54

The Motionless Statue

Phase 1. Spin one child around, and then have him or her freeze in one position and pretend to be a statue. The "statue" is to stand totally still except for blinking his or her eyes. Then give each member of the class the same amount of time to try to get the statue to move (without touching him or her). Any movement other than normal eye blinking disqualifies the child as the statue. The student who can stand still the longest is the winner.

Phase 2. In more advanced classes, allow students to select the position in which they wish to "freeze."

EXERCISE 55

Make the Sad Child Laugh

In this contest, give each student an opportunity to play a sad child who doesn't laugh anymore. Give each member of the class an equal amount of time to try to make the sad child laugh (again, no touching). The student who can last the longest without laughing is the winner. The member of the class who is able to make the sad child laugh is also a winner.

Character Control

The exercises in this section help students learn to concentrate on a particular type of character and to be consistent with the character in front of the group.

EXERCISE 56

Costume Bag

Put articles of clothing into a large bag. Each item of clothing should suggest a particular type of character. Good items for this exercise include a black cape, a shawl, a top hat, an apron, jewelry, a crown, a feather boa, a cane, dark glasses, a motorcycle helmet, knitting needles, a gypsy turban, a sheriff's badge, etc.

Have the students get up two at a time, reach into the bag, and each select one item. Then tell the children to think about the type of characters that would either wear the item they selected or use it as a prop. Allow each pair time to briefly discuss their characters and invent a simple situation ("skit") that involves the two characters together; then have them perform their situation in front of the class.

Because this is a very popular and effective exercise, try to allow each pair several turns performing as their characters.

EXERCISE 57

Act Out the Name

Divide the class into pairs. Give each partner a name that suggests a particular personality, and then let each pair invent a simple situation (such as sitting on a park bench) involving their characters. The object is to carry on a conversation while each partner maintains the type of character given to him or her.

Here are some examples of characters: the big cry-baby, the fast-talker, the snob, the silly one, the nervous one, the shy one, the brat, the old person, the slow talker, the crank, and the happy one.

EXERCISE 58

Fairy Tale Character

Have the students think of their favorite fairy tale, folk, or comic book characters. Then have them concentrate on a unique trait that makes their favorite character much different from other characters.

When they are ready, have the children portray their characters in front of the group. The object of the exercise is to see if the class can guess what character is being portrayed. If the class is unable to determine the character, discuss why, and help the student simplify his or her character and make it more distinctive. Then have the student repeat the portrayal, this time including the suggestions.

From *Creative Dramatics for Children* by Maureen McCurry Cresci © 1989 Scott, Foresman and Company.

Likely characters for this exercise include Snow White, Spiderman, Aladdin, King Midas, Cinderella, Rip Van Winkle, Alice in Wonderland, Tiny Tim, Paul Bunyan, Old Mother Hubbard, the Pied Piper, and Little Red Riding Hood.

Extending the Activities to Other Areas of the Curriculum

WRITING

After they complete Exercise 48, have the children write about an experience or event in two different ways, presenting the points of view of two different characters. For example, have them write about giving a dog a bath, first from the viewpoint of the dog and then from that of the groomer.

Use exercises 57 and 58 to stimulate a writing activity that focuses on detailed descriptions of characters. Encourage the students to describe in writing exactly how a character looks, moves, acts, etc.

After they complete Exercise 58, have the students write stories that involve a character from one fairy or folk tale appearing in another one—e.g., "Cinderella Meets Little Red Riding Hood."

ART

After they complete Exercise 52, Phase 2, have the students experiment with drawing pictures of faces with different expressions. See if they can draw faces that clearly express worry, greed, satisfaction, etc.

Following Exercise 57, see if the students can illustrate the character types by finding and cutting out pictures from magazines. Then have them work in groups to assemble their pictures into a character collage or mural.

SOCIAL STUDIES

Incorporate Exercise 56 into your current social studies unit by choosing costume articles and props that reflect careers, countries, or cultures that you are studying. You could include, for example, a microscope, a chef's hat, a Japanese tea pot, etc.

Use Exercise 57 to stimulate a discussion about stereotypes or the effects of labeling on people. Ask students if they have ever been labeled and how they felt about it. Then talk about labeling others—individuals or groups.

In Exercise 58, try substituting real characters from history—Napoleon, Betsy Ross, King Henry VIII, Susan B. Anthony, etc.—for the fairy tale, folk tale, and comic book characters.

The goals of this group of exercises are to give the children confidence in speaking in front of a group, practice in speaking clearly and distinctly, and experience with different kinds of extemporaneous speeches.

Introducing the Exercises to Your Students

Ask your students to close their eyes and recall a time when they listened to someone who they thought was a good speaker. Encourage them to identify and share with the class what techniques or qualities made that person speak so well.

Then ask the class: "Do actors need to develop speaking skills, too? Why?" Explain that the following activities will help them to develop the qualities they identified with effective speaking—and do so in a very enjoyable way!

Vocal and Speech Variation Exercises

EXERCISE 59

Vocal Projection

Divide the class into pairs. Then give each pair one of the following situations, all of which require the students to speak very clearly and loudly to one another.

Suggested Situations:

A person in a small boat asking for directions from a person aboard a large ship.

A person lost in an underground tunnel; a person somewhere underground trying to find the lost person.

Two people together in a blizzard, trying to find shelter and food.

A person in an upstairs window, calling to a friend in the street.

Two people talking long distance on the phone, trying to make themselves understood over a lot of static on the line.

Two people—both of whom are *very* hard of hearing—who haven't seen each other in years.

A person on the ground asking for directions from a person at the top of a lighthouse.

A job foreman on the ground giving directions to a worker using a large construction machine.

Two people in the audience at a rock concert, trying to carry on a conversation.

EXERCISE 60

One Sentence Said Different Ways

This is an excellent exercise to help students see clearly and make use of a variety of ways to deliver lines to an audience.

Phase 1. Give each student a slip of paper with a simple sentence written on it (a different sentence for every student). Have the students, one at a time, read their sentence in the following ways:

1. As they would normally.
2. As a news announcer would.
3. As someone would who didn't understand the meaning of the sentence.
4. As someone would who finds the sentence very sad.
5. As someone would who finds the sentence very funny.

Phase 2. Give the students new sentences to read in different ways, this time according to the emotional states listed below.

1. Happy
2. Angry
3. Excited
4. Nervous

The following are some examples of sentences you can use for this exercise. You may use the same sentences in Phase 2 as in Phase 1, but be sure that every student has different sentences to read.

I went for a walk the other day and fell down.

Last night my dog bit me on the end of my nose.

I wondered how long it would take before you said that.

I had to walk seven blocks to catch the school bus.

My mother wears a different colored wig every day.

Last night my parrot told me to leave the house.

My bathtub is so big that I can swim in it.

Yesterday I decided to start taking driving lessons.

It takes my father three hours to walk around the golf course.

Today I decided to eat 17 daisies for lunch.

I did the dishes last night and broke two cups and one glass.

Yesterday I bought a new sweater, but today my dog ate it.

I climbed a tree yesterday and stayed there all night.

Last night I fixed dinner for the whole family in five minutes.

Cold Readings

The students are to read the following commercials together, two or three at a time depending on how many characters are in the script. Be sure to have enough copies of the script prepared for all the students participating in the exercise.

   Give each child an opportunity to read through the script before reading it aloud so that the student can get answers to any questions he or she may have about the script. Allow each set of students to read the commercial two or three times in front of the group. Between readings, make suggestions that will help them in re-reading the script.

EXERCISE 61

Toothpaste
(Two Characters)

(Two children on their way to school)
1. (Running to catch the other) Hey, wait!
2. Well . . . hurry up. You'll make us both late!

1. (Panting) Thanks. Mom made me go back and brush my teeth with that awful "green" stuff.
2. What "green" stuff?
1. The toothpaste that is supposed to keep you from getting cavities.
2. Tastes pretty bad, huh?
1. Yes. Just awful.

From *Creative Dramatics for Children* by Maureen McCurry Cresci © 1989 Scott, Foresman and Company.

2. Why don't you get your Mom to buy "Sparkle Plenty" toothpaste? It's just as good for your teeth, and it tastes really *great.*
1. "Sparkle Plenty"?
2. Yep . . . . Let's hurry or we'll really be late!
1. Oh! Sure!

EXERCISE 62

Flea Collar
(Two Characters)

(Two children playing with a dog)
1. (Looking at the dog) Ralph sure is a terrific looking dog!
2. He's been looking really sad lately. I just can't figure it out.
1. (Patting the dog) Hey, what's the matter big boy?
2. He seems worried about something. Scratches himself all the time, too.

1. (Looking at the other child in amazement) If he's scratching himself, he's telling you something.
2. Huh?
1. The old boy has fleas. (Talking to the dog) Isn't that right, Ralph? . . . (Pointing to a flea) Just look at that; they're murdering him!
2. (Suddenly looking very worried) No kidding?
1. Haven't you ever heard of Majors Flea Collars?
2. Sure, but I never thought that old Ralph had FLEAS!
1. Come on, let's go get a flea collar for the old boy.
2. OK! (Leaning over and hugging Ralph) Want to come along, Ralph?

EXERCISE 63

Plant Food
(Two Characters)

(Two children looking at a plant)
1. Hey! Isn't that the plant I gave you for your birthday?
2. Sure is!
1. What did you DO to it?
2. Nothing. I can't understand what's happening to it.
1. Forget to water it?
2. NO! I water it two times a week . . . . I PROMISE!
1. It looks like you *walked* on it!
2. Thanks a lot.
1. Why don't you try some "Always Green" plant food? Mom uses it all the time, and you know how pretty HER plants are.
2. Where does she get it?
1. I think you can get it just about ANYWHERE.
2. Well, let's go get some. I really like this plant. Let's see if "Always Green" can do the job.
(Both children leave)

EXERCISE 64

Yogurt
(Three Characters)

(1 wants what 2 is eating)
1. I'll give you a dime.
2. (Shakes head) Nope.
1. (Looking hopeful) I'll give you a frog.
2. (Thinking) Nope.
1. I'll give you all my baseball cards.
2. Well . . . no, I don't think so.
1. I'll do your homework for you tonight.
2. You will?
1. Yes, I will. I really will.
2. Cross your heart? You really will?
1. Yes. I will.
2. (Thinking carefully) Nah! It's still not fair. (Starts eating the yogurt out of the container)
Announcer: There are some things a person just will not trade. Smith's Yogurt is truly delicious. Try one of the many wonderful flavors. You'll agree. You wouldn't trade it for anything either!

EXERCISE 65

Maple Syrup
(Three Characters)

(Two people at the breakfast table, eating hot cakes)
1. Why do you smile every time you take a bite?
2. Secret.
1. You and your secrets! Who cares, anyway.
2. (Long pause) YOU.
1. OK . . . Why are you smiling?
2. It's the syrup. Aunt Mary's. You're just using butter on your hot cakes. This syrup is fantastic.
1. Oh, yeah? Pass it over. I'll try it. (Pours on syrup)

2. Well?
1. I haven't tried it yet. (Takes a big bite) Wow!
2. Every time I share a secret you use it all up. Please don't use all the Aunt Mary's!
1. I didn't! Look there's plenty left. (Smiling very broadly) Boy, this syrup is REALLY good!
Announcer: Good maple syrup can make *anyone* smile. Aunt Mary's Maple Syrup is truly the best. Put some on your pancakes today, and you'll be smiling too.

EXERCISE 66

Coffee
(Three Characters)

(Husband and wife eating at a table)
Wife: Here's a piece of my best cake, dear.
Husband: Great cake as usual, honey . . . (Takes a sip of coffee, makes a face) And the coffee is "as usual" too.
(The next day: Wife and neighbor drinking coffee at table)
Wife: Oh Marge, what can I do? Steve just hates my coffee!
Neighbor: No problem! Coffee is always delicious when you use "Rolling Hills." That's because it's mountain grown.
Wife: Mountain grown?
Neighbor: That's right. Also vacuum packed, so the flavor stays in. Good coffee every time.
Wife: Oh, thanks Marge! You're a REAL friend!
(Later that same day: Husband and wife at table)
Husband: (Taking a sip of coffee) This coffee is great! What did you do to it?
Wife: You are drinking "Rolling Hills Mountain Grown Coffee." Do you *really* like it?
Husband: It's delicious! As a matter of fact, it's as good as your cake!
(They both laugh)

From *Creative Dramatics for Children* by Maureen McCurry Cresci © 1989 Scott, Foresman and Company.

EXERCISE 67

Ballpoint Pen
(Two Characters)

(Two children walking home from school)
1. What are your folks going to say when they see the grade on your English report?
2. I don't know. It wasn't my fault, anyway.
1. Oh?
2. It really wasn't my fault. My pen ran out of ink!
1. Gee, that's rough. The pen I got for my birthday never has run out. It's an "Everlife," the best you can buy.
2. Did you write your report with it?
1. Yes.
2. What grade did you get on your report?
1. An "A."
2. If I had an "Everlife Pen," I would get "A's" all the time too.
1. I doubt it!
(Looking angry, 2 chases after 1)

EXERCISE 68

Fruit Juice
(Three Characters)

(Two children sitting at kitchen table)
1. Well, there's nothing like a good old soft drink!
2. Yeah. There's nothing like the way your face is breaking out from "good old soft drinks."
1. That's not making my face break out!
2. If you started drinking "Fresh Fruit Juice" instead, I'll bet your face would clear up.
(Several days later)
2. Hey! You look great!
1. Thanks! By the way, I stopped drinking

soft drinks and started drinking "Fresh Fruit Juice." My skin is all cleared up.
2. Why do you suppose that happened?
1. All the sugar in the soft drinks?
2. Right! It's bad for your skin.
1. Thanks for the tip.
Announcer: Be good to *your* skin. Drink "Fresh Fruit Juice." Have you ever seen a fruit tree with soft drink bottles growing on it? Nature just may be trying to tell us something!

EXERCISE 69

Keep the City Clean
(Two Characters)

(Two children walking down the street)
1. Don't you EVER get sick of eating candy?
2. Nope.
1. Can I have a bite?
2. Nope.
1. That's really mean. Why can't I have just ONE little bite?
2. (Laughing) It's all gone now! (Crumples up the candy wrapper and throws it on the sidewalk)
1. Hey! What did you do that for?
2. What?
1. Throw the paper down on the sidewalk?(Picks up paper, walks to trash can, and throws it away) People who throw paper in the street make the city dirty.
2. I never thought about it like that. (Looks very guilty) I guess that I should start being more careful.
1. Yes. We should ALL try to keep our streets clean.
2. I'll start by putting candy wrappers in the trash from now on.
1. That's a good idea for ALL of us.
(They continue walking down the street)

EXERCISE 70

Spray Starch
(Two Characters)

(Two children standing by an ironing board)
1. What are you doing?
2. Getting ready to scream! Mom said I had to iron my shirt. It looks all limp and old.
1. Did you spray any "Puff" on it?
2. What's "Puff"?
1. Spray starch. It makes all clothes "come back to life" again. I'll go get some now. (Leaves room, and then returns holding can) Here. Try it!
2. (Sprays and irons) Hey, look! My shirt is starting to look like new again!
1. Mom uses "Puff" on everything!
2. (Finished with ironing and holding up shirt) Look! My shirt looks just great. It looks like new.
1. It sure does. "Puff" works like magic!
2. Thanks a lot.
1. (Smiling) Anytime!

EXERCISE 71

Cough Tablets
(Two Characters)

(Two children lying in bed)
1. My throat hurts.
2. You *would* get sick tonight of all nights . . . when Mom and Dad are at the movies.
1. I can't help it.
2. Do you think you're going to be REAL sick?
1. I don't know. I have a sore throat.
2. (Reaching beside the bed) What about these "Evergreen Cough Tablets"? They helped me a lot when I got sick.
1. (Opens box and takes a tablet) Gee! They taste good!
2. (Pause) How's your throat?

1. It feels a little better. I think I'll be OK. The tablet is starting to work already!
2. Good. With "Evergreen Cough Tablets" and some sleep, you'll be good as new tomorrow!
1. Thanks. Good night.
2. Good night.

EXERCISE 72

Laundry Soap
(Two Characters)

(Two children in the laundry room)
1. How come you have to do the laundry?
2. Mom doesn't feel good.
1. Well, I guess that means that we can't go to the park.
2. Why did you say that?
1. Well, you'll be here all day measuring out the soap.
2. No I won't. Not with "Rave." All I have to do is drop these two little tablets in and I'm done!
1. Really? Is that soap really good?
2. Mom says that it's the best! (Starts to walk away)
1. Are you finished?
2. Sure. Come on, let's go to the park!
1. "Rave" really makes things easy!
2. It sure does!

EXERCISE 73

Bug Spray
(Two Characters)

(Two children in sleeping bags)
1. Ouch!
2. What's wrong?
1. I'm being eaten alive. Bugs are crawling on me and eating me alive!

2. My Dad was right. He said it would work.
1. What would work?
2. Forget it. I'm tired. Go to sleep.
1. I can't. The bugs are killing me. What did you say about your Dad?
2. He gave me some bug spray. He told me to spray it around my sleeping bag. I haven't felt ONE single bug!
1. What kind of spray?
2. It's called "Zap."
1. Is there any left?
2. Sure. Take the rest of it. (Hands the can to friend) I would do *anything* to get some sleep.
1. (Sprays ground) OK, "ZAP" do your stuff! (Crawls back into sleeping bag) Good night.
2. Good night.

EXERCISE 74

Spot Remover
(Two Characters)

(Two children sitting on the floor, painting pictures)
1. Maybe if this is good enough, I can sell it!
2. It's really pretty. You probably could!
1. Yours is pretty too. I like the color of red.
2. Oh no!
1. What's wrong?
2. I got some paint on your mother's carpet.
1. What color?
2. Red. Can't you see? It's all red!
1. I'll get the "Zipp."
2. What's "Zipp"?
1. Spot remover. It takes all stains out. (Runs out of room)
2. Hurry!
(1 returns with bottle and pours it on carpet)
2. It's coming out!
1. I told you! See? It's all gone!
2. Gee, that really works!

1. Mom uses "Zipp" on everything. Now let's take our paintings outside to dry. (Picks up painting)
2. Good idea. (Picks up picture)

EXERCISE 75

Peanut Butter
(Two Characters)

(Two children home from school for lunch)
1. (Looking at a note) Oh, no!
2. What?
1. (Picking up the note and reading) It's a note from Mom. She says, "Sorry, I have an important meeting. You two will have to fix your own lunches."
2. What will we fix?
1. I'm going to make a "Nutty Peanut Butter" sandwich.
2. Is it any good?
1. It's terrific! Come on, let's make some sandwiches.
(Both busy themselves making sandwiches, then sit down to eat)
2. This peanut butter is really wonderful.
1. That's because there are both nuts and raisins in new "Nutty Peanut Butter"!
2. Delicious.

EXERCISE 76

Pimple Cream
(Two Characters)

(Two sisters in their bedroom)
1. (Sitting in front of mirror) Oh, look! This is terrible! (Starts to cry)
2. What happened? Why are you crying?
1. Look! A great big giant pimple. Steve asked me to go to the movies. I have a new skirt, and my hair looks great, but I have a great big giant pimple right on the end of my nose. (Shows sister)
2. (Looks at sister) That's terrible. (Very concerned) You're not going to believe this, but your only sister is going to save you!
1. (Looking surprised) How can you "save" me?
2. With "Medicated Constant Cover Up." It hides the blemish, and it also makes it go away. (Hands sister the tube)
1. (Puts on some cream) I can't see the pimple. It's gone!
2. It's hidden now, but it will be gone tomorrow!
1. "Constant Cover Up," you are wonderful! (Turns to sister) And you are wonderful too. Thank you!
2. Any time!

EXERCISE 77

Dog Food
(Two Characters)

(Two children in a house)
1. (Walking into friend's house) Hi! Where are the puppies?
2. Over there in the corner. In the big box.
1. (Picking up a puppy) They're really cute! Can I have this one?
2. I think my cousin wants that one.

1. (Looking sad and putting puppy down) Oh.
2. The one with the black spots is cuter, though. If I could keep one, I think that's the one I would keep. You can have him.
1. Really? (Picks up puppy and looks at it) Well, hi there fella!
2. Make sure you feed him "Grow a Lot" dog food. It's supposed to be the very best.
1. "Grow a Lot"?
2. Yes. It helps the puppy grow up to be big and strong.
1. (Talking to puppy) By the time you are big enough to come home with me, I'll have lots of "Grow a Lot" dog food for you at home.
2. He understood what you said! See? He wagged his tail!

EXERCISE 78

Tennis Shoes
(Two Characters)

(Two children playing tennis)
1. Here comes another ball.
2. (Misses) Oops!
1. That's the eighth one that you've missed. You keep sliding all over like an ice skater.
2. I'm doing my best! I'm really doing my best!
1. Your feet! I think it's your feet!
2. What? What's wrong with my feet?
1. Are you wearing "Leap" tennis shoes?
2. No. Just an old pair.
1. Look. (Points at feet) These are "Leaps." They stop you in your tracks and help you jump higher. Every tennis player should wear them!
2. You're probably right. Let's quit for now. I'll get some new "Leaps" and meet you here tomorrow!
(The next day, after the game)
1. That was a terrific game!

2. Thanks to your advice and my new "Leaps" tennis shoes!
1. With "Leaps" on your feet, you're playing tennis like an expert!
(They walk off arm in arm)

EXERCISE 79

Pain Spray
(Two Characters)

1. (Runs into house, holding knee)
2. What happened?

1. I fell down and skinned my knee . . . real bad!
2. Oh. That looks awful. Does it hurt?
1. (Whimpering) Yes, a lot!
2. Let's see what we can find in the bathroom. (They walk into the bathroom and open the medicine cabinet) Here's a can of "All Better Pain Spray."
1. (Holding knee) I hope it doesn't burn!
2. It doesn't. It's not like the old kind of spray.
1. (Wincing) Well, we should probably try it. (Makes a terrible face, waiting for the spray to burn)
2. (Sprays knee) Did it hurt?
1. No. (They both laugh) It really is "All Better"!

Impromptu Speech and Storytelling

EXERCISE 80

One Object—Tell a Story

Phase 1. Sit in a circle with all of the students, and place an object in the middle. Tell the class to think very carefully about what the object might be and where it might have come from. Then ask each child to tell his or her own little original story about the object.

For this exercise, it is best to use objects likely to stimulate the imagination—e.g., a sea shell, a candle and candleholder, marbles, a piece of driftwood, decorative art objects, a kerosene lantern, pieces of jewelry, nature items, etc.

Phase 2. Give all the students different objects, and tell them to invent an original

story about their object. For this exercise, it is a good idea to have students deliver their stories soon after receiving their objects and to give back the objects immediately after telling their tales. Otherwise, they may play with the objects and not listen attentively to others in the class.

EXERCISE 81

Continue the Story

Phase 1. Sit in a circle with all of the students. Start telling a story, or choose one of the students to start telling it. Designate one person to clap hands when the storyteller is to stop talking. The story then

From *Creative Dramatics for Children* by Maureen McCurry Cresci © 1989 Scott, Foresman and Company.

goes around the circle, with each person adding to it, every time the designated person claps hands.

Phase 2. Give each student a different object (e.g., a marble, a piece of string, a button), and then follow the procedure outlined in Phase 1. This time, however, the student must introduce his or her object into the story.

Phase 3. Again, follow the procedure outlined in Phase 1, but this time have each student introduce a living creature of some kind into the continuing story when his or her turn comes around.

EXERCISE 82

Prop Bag

This exercise requires a large fabric bag with loose elastic at the top. A bag made of brightly colored fabric is very effective.

Find and put into the bag a variety of objects that children would find stimulating. Here are some suggestions: a big paper flower, a clock, a silver dish, a picture in a frame, a frame with no picture, a hammer, a piggy bank, fuzzy bedroom slippers, a sock with a big hole in it, a light bulb. Be prepared with a large number of objects; children enjoy doing this exercise as many times as possible.

Have each child close his or her eyes and pick an object from the bag. After selecting their objects, the children are to be quiet for a few minutes to think about what the object means to them. After thinking about their objects, the children may do anything they want with the items. They may tell a story, "sell" the item to someone else in the class, or use the object in such a manner that the rest of the group understands what new meaning the child has given to the object and what the object has become in the child's imagination.

EXERCISE 83

Commercials from Objects in Pillowcase

Put a number of household products into a pillowcase—e.g., floor wax, shampoo, tea bags, shoe polish, dog soap, cat food. Divide the class into pairs, and have one partner from each pair reach into the pillowcase and select a product.

Tell the students to create a small situation that could be used as the basis for a brief commercial. Give them several minutes to discuss their situations, and then have them pretend that they are on television performing their commercials.

EXERCISE 84

Speech—"I'd like to tell you about the day that I . . . ."

Start this exercise (as well as 85-87) by introducing each speaker as a "Very Important Person." Explain that the VIP will deliver a speech on the given subject and that after the speech the class will be free to ask the speaker questions on the subject of the speech.

Here are some suggestions for subjects that go with "I would like to tell you about the day that I . . . ." Students may draw their subjects from a hat, or you can tell each student the specific topic of his or her speech.

- captured a bank robber.
- was aboard a hijacked plane to Cuba.
- saved my sister's life.
- discovered that I could fly all by myself.
- won the Academy Award for Best Actor or Best Actress.

- fought off four man-eating sharks.
- boarded a plane for Los Angeles and ended up in Japan.
- told my parents that I was being put back a grade.
- discovered that I could predict the future.
- was kissed by my favorite rock star.
- told my parents that I wanted to become a professional belly dancer.
- spent the evening with Santa Claus.
- discovered that I had "X-ray vision."
- won a million dollars in a television contest.
- was talked to by a tree.
- could become invisible just by saying "Zap."

EXERCISE 85

Speech—"I'd like to tell the class how to . . . ."

Follow the general procedure presented in Exercise 84, but use the suggestions below for subjects to go with "I'd like to tell the class how to . . . ."

- milk a cow.
- change a diaper.
- change a tire on a steep hill in the snow.
- catch 12 frogs in 12 minutes.
- babysit for 10 children.
- make it rain.
- make it stop raining.
- make a kite out of tissue paper.
- stay alive on a raft for three months.
- prune a rose bush in the dark.
- build a house out of rocks.
- make a coat out of tree bark.
- use a skateboard on the hills of San Francisco.
- rob a bank in a gorilla costume.
- become a rock star in three weeks.
- train a baby elephant.

- keep an alligator as a pet.
- make a 10-foot tall wedding cake in a small kitchen.
- start a fire with two sticks, in the rain.
- make friends with a fierce bear.
- train a kitten to use a litter box.
- teach a parrot to talk.

EXERCISE 86

Speech—"Why I decided to . . . ."

Follow the general procedure presented in Exercise 84, but use the suggestions below for subjects to go with "Why I decided to . . . ."

- join the circus.
- cultivate worms in my garden.
- never get married.
- paint pictures with my toes.
- shave my head.
- eat only apples and peanuts.
- be a professional tap dancer.
- become President of the United States.
- gain 200 pounds.
- wear a jeweled turban.
- sleep in a garage from now on.
- never wear shoes again.
- live in a tree.

EXERCISE 87

Speech—"I am the authority on . . . ."

Ask the students to pretend that they are at a dinner meeting of a club to which they all belong. The club has invited several guest speakers to give talks on different subjects. Each student is to make a speech on a subject that you give him or her immediately before he or she gets up to talk.

Tell the students that they should act as though they know what they are talking about while their audience knows nothing on the subject. Since they are the "authority," they may say anything they like on the topic. Instruct the class to applaud before and after every speech.

Here are some suggestions to go with "I am the authority on . . . ."

* polar bears.
* ghosts.
* dinosaurs.
* bats.
* Santa Claus.
* building blocks.
* mud pies.
* the tooth fairy.
* bubble gum.
* tightrope walking.
* alligators.
* giant African frogs.
* training fleas.
* brain surgery.
* space travel.
* exotic flowers.
* elves.
* life on other planets.
* staying happily married.
* traveling around the world inexpensively.
* living on a rubber raft.

EXERCISE 88
Debate With a Partner

This exercise is very good for helping students develop mental flexibility and the ability to create new thoughts quickly while working with a partner.

Phase 1. Divide the class into pairs, and give each pair a simple topic of conversation. Tell one partner in each pair to argue in favor of the topic while the other partner argues against it. The argument should take the form of a true conversation, with each partner creating actual sentences that pertain to the topic. In the middle of the exercise, have the partners change sides.

Appropriate topics for this exercise include wigs, shoes, rain, mice, kissing, poodles, gambling, crying, movies, air pollution, candy, rock and roll, and telephones.

Phase 2. Cast each student as a specific character type, and then have the partners debate while each maintains the assigned character.

EXERCISE 89
Convince Your Partner

Phase 1. Divide the class into pairs, and give each pair a situation in which one person tries to convince or persuade the partner to agree about a particular subject. The partner must keep coming up with reasons for not agreeing. Allow the students to talk until one side has obviously become stronger than the other. Then have the partners switch sides.

Here are a couple of suggestions of situations that are appropriate for this exercise. Convince your partner that . . . .

* you are the best actor or actress in the class.
* you are never going to laugh again.

Phase 2. Cast the partners in the roles specified in the situation suggestions below. Then follow the procedure presented in Phase 1.

Convince your . . . .

- teacher that you should get a better grade.
- brother/sister that he/she should stop sharing your room and sleep in the basement instead.

- mother that she should grow all her own vegetables.
- father that you are old enough to drive the family car.
- father/mother that you are old enough to date.

Extending the Activities to Other Areas of the Curriculum

WRITING

After doing Exercise 60, have your students write short stories, using the sentences as titles. Encourage more than one student to use the same title but to write about it in a different way. For example, two students may write about "I have to walk seven blocks"—one creating a happy story and the other writing an angry one.

In conjunction with exercises 61 through 79 or with 83, have your students write their own scripts for product commercials. Let them work in pairs or small groups and invent their own lines, but make it clear that the writing must be done in script form.

Also in association with exercises 61-79 and 83, have your students study product ads in magazines and then discuss the writing techniques utilized in advertising copy. Let them write some of their own print ads for real or imaginary products.

After they complete Exercise 84, encourage your students to write about "The Most Unusual Day I Ever Had." Tell the students that they may use the sentences suggested in the exercise or invent their own wild situations.

ART

After doing Exercise 81 and making sure that the students are comfortable with it, repeat it on another day and tape record the "chain story." Later, divide the story into sections (about six to eight), and transcribe the sections onto large pieces of posterboard. Then have your students work in small groups to illustrate the story. You can place the illustrated pieces of posterboard on the wall in sequence to create a mural story, or you can even fasten them together into a giant "book."

In conjunction with the third writing activity (writing advertising copy), have your students pay special attention to the graphic designs and illustrations they find in the magazine product ads. Then have them create their own designs and illustrations to go with their original ads. They can even create a logo for their product, too.

After they complete Exercise 85, have the children pick a "how to" and illustrate the procedure in a sequence of drawings. Encourage them to use as few words as possible.

SOCIAL STUDIES

Take exercises 61 through 79 and 83 (the advertising activities) a step further by having a discussion about the importance of advertising in our culture and economy. Bring in a variety of ads and ask your students to figure out what persuasive techniques each ad uses. If possible, ask a representative from a local advertising agency to come to your classroom and discuss careers in advertising with your students.

Adapt Exercise 84 to the country your students are learning about in social studies—e.g., "The day I woke up in China (or Brazil, Ghana, etc.)."

SCIENCE

When doing Exercise 80 (Phases 1 and 2), use objects from nature or objects associated with a career in science (a test tube, dental tool, geology pick, etc.).

In Exercise 85, give your students topics that include some scientific information—e.g., How to grow (or How *not* to grow) your own garden; How to care for your pet.

PART 4
IMPROVISATIONAL WORK

The improvisations in this part require the use of all of the skills presented in the previous activities. Far more than those previous activities, however, the following exercises develop the students' ability to work spontaneously and to call upon their own creative imaginations.

Introducing the Exercises to Your Students

Ask the students if they know what the word "improvisation" means, and then discuss their answers. Explain that professional actors use improvisations as part of their training.

Tell them that the key elements in doing improvisations are spontaneity and creativity. There are no rules or correct way to perform, except that they must stay within the given situation. How long an improvisation goes depends on how long it takes to reach a satisfactory resolution of the situation and how long the performance holds the audience's interest.

42

From *Creative Dramatics for Children* by Maureen McCurry Cresci © 1989 Scott, Foresman and Company.

Improvisations

The following simple improvisational situations are intended for students to work on in pairs. They are supposed to act out what they would do or say in each given set of circumstances. Remind them to face the audience, enunciate clearly, and keep in mind that they are performing a miniature play.

Some students prefer having a brief time to prepare before performing while others enjoy being totally spontaneous. After a bit of experimentation, you'll discover the method that best suits your group.

EXERCISE 90

You have spent the day collecting butterflies for a school assignment. You walk into your bedroom just as your brother or sister is letting them go free out the window.

EXERCISE 91

Your brother or sister has just built a clubhouse. You want to use it for a slumber party with four of your friends. Your parents agree to let you have the party if your brother or sister agrees to let you use the clubhouse. You discuss the situation with your sibling.

EXERCISE 92

You are applying for a job in a bakery even though you don't know anything about the bakery business. You try very hard to get the job.

EXERCISE 93

Your mother has worked very hard sewing a new dress for you to wear to a party. When you try it on, though, you don't like it. Trying hard not to hurt your mother's feelings, you explain why you won't wear the dress.

EXERCISE 94

A friend of yours has arranged for you to go on a blind date. When you meet your date, you instantly decide that you don't want to go out with him/her. But the date thinks you are wonderful. What do you say to each other?

EXERCISE 95

You have received a scholarship to go to art school. Your father wants you to drop out of school and go into the laundry business with him. What do you say?

EXERCISE 96

You are being interviewed for a job as a clown. You are trying to be very funny and witty, but the person interviewing you has no sense of humor.

EXERCISE 97

Your mother kept her favorite plant on a table in the living room. This afternoon you were playing ball in the house, and the plant was ruined. She asks you where her plant is. What do you say?

EXERCISE 98

You are dressed up as a burglar for a costume party; but you get lost on your way to the party, and you are discovered wandering around someone's back yard.

EXERCISE 99

You have asked a girl/boy to go with you to a special party, and you are all dressed up. When you arrive at her/his house, however, you see that she/he has misunderstood. She/he is wearing jeans and a sweater.

EXERCISE 100

Your friend, remembering that it's your birthday, brings you a kitten as a gift. You don't like cats, but you don't want to hurt your friend's feelings. What do you say?

EXERCISE 101

You are on an airplane, terrified of flying. The person sitting next to you insists upon talking a lot about airplane crashes.

EXERCISE 102

You're in a big hurry at the grocery store as you stand in the check-out line with two bags of groceries. But you can't find your money. What do you say and do?

EXERCISE 103

You are sitting on a park bench enjoying the sun. A person sits down beside you and wants to stretch out and put his/her head in your lap.

EXERCISE 104

You deliver newspapers. Every time you try to collect from a certain house, the people there tell you to come back another time. Your boss has told you that you must get the money from them today. What do you say to the people?

EXERCISE 105

Your friend throws a rock that breaks a window, and then he runs away. The owner of the house comes outside and accuses *you* of breaking his window.

EXERCISE 106

You feel that you were given an unfair grade on a test because the teacher doesn't like you. What do you say to the teacher?

EXERCISE 107

You are alone on a beach until a person sits down on a blanket next to you and turns on a loud radio.

EXERCISE 108

You are sitting in your room doing your homework when a burglar suddenly climbs in the window. It is someone you know.

EXERCISE 109

Your best friend has been copying your work at school. You are afraid that both of you will get in trouble. What do you say to your friend?

EXERCISE 110

Your wealthy grandfather has died and left you a lot of money. Your mother/father tells you that you should give the money away to the poor. You have just received the check. What do you say to your parent?

EXERCISE 111

You have called your cousin long distance. Your cousin won't stop talking. You see your phone bill rising higher and higher.

EXERCISE 112

You have just bought your first car. Just after the warranty expires, you can see that something is very wrong with the engine. You go to talk with the person who sold you the car.

EXERCISE 113

You are moving to a new town today. Your best friend comes to your house to say good-bye. Although you are looking forward to your new home, both you and your friend are sad. What do you say?

EXERCISE 114

Your aunt/uncle, whom you have never met, is coming over for a visit. You answer the door to find that your relative is a famous movie star.

EXERCISE 115

You have just found a kitten that you want to keep. Your mother isn't interested in having a pet. Try to persuade her that the kitten needs you.

EXERCISE 116

A person selling vacuum cleaners comes to the door. Although you already own a vacuum cleaner, the salesperson insists on demonstrating his/her model in your house. What do you do?

EXERCISE 117

Without first getting his/her permission, you wore your brother's/sister's expensive watch to a picnic and lost it. How do you tell him/her what happened?

EXERCISE 118

You are walking down the street and see a $20 bill on the ground. You need the money. Just then you see someone walking around looking for something. What do you say to the person? What does the person say to you?

EXERCISE 119

You have always been a big bully. Your mother/father warned you that if you were in one more fight you would get no allowance for a month. Tonight you got hit in the face with a softball, and you have a black eye. Try to explain to your mother/father how you got the black eye.

EXERCISE 120

Your friend has decided to drop out of school and go to work full time. You try to talk your friend into staying in school.

EXERCISE 121

Though nominated for "The Nicest Person In School," you lost by one vote. Now you find out that your little brother/sister voted against you. The two of you are alone. What do you say?

EXERCISE 122

A close friend of yours is getting friendly with a very rough crowd. You think that you can talk some sense into your friend's head.

EXERCISE 123

Your aunt/uncle is an actress/actor. You are anxious to get into show business. She/he wants to discourage you.

EXERCISE 124

You are alone at home, and someone knocks at the door. It is the neighbor who is always borrowing your things. He/she wants to borrow something that you use a lot.

EXERCISE 125

You wake up in the hospital. The person standing beside your bed says that you are his/her brother/sister. You don't remember anything, including ever seeing this person before.

EXERCISE 126

You are crawling across the desert with another person. You ask the other person for some water. While you weren't looking, this person drank it all.

EXERCISE 127

You have been assigned a roommate at boarding school. When you walk into your room for the first time to meet this person, you find that the room already has been turned into a big mess.

EXERCISE 128

Your mother has a new boyfriend. You don't like him much, and you are afraid that she is getting serious about him. Tell her how you feel.

EXERCISE 129

Your father has been transferred to another city. You don't want to move and leave your friends. Tell your father that you want to stay and live with your aunt and uncle.

EXERCISE 130

You are driving to the hospital to visit someone who is very sick. A cranky policeman who doesn't like young drivers stops you for speeding.

EXERCISE 131

You have been kidnapped. You are alone with the son/daughter of the kidnapper. This is your only chance to try to talk him/her into letting you go.

EXERCISE 132

Your little brother/sister has just been told that there is no Santa *or* Easter Bunny. What do you say to him/her?

EXERCISE 133

You and your friend have had a fight. Although you want to be friends again, he/she doesn't seem interested. What do you say to each other when you meet by accident after school?

EXERCISE 134

You have just inherited $5,000. You want to donate it to a worthy cause, but your mother/father thinks that you should save the money for school.

EXERCISE 135

When one of your friends comes to your home with a Christmas gift, you suddenly remember that you didn't get a gift for your friend.

EXERCISE 136

One of your friends borrowed your new sweater. When you get it back, you find that it has ink stains on it. What do you say to your friend?

EXERCISE 137

You had some money in your coat pocket and now it is missing. You find your brother/sister, who was broke earlier in the day, gulping down two hamburgers.

Improvisational Exercises

EXERCISE 138

Improvisations from Objects in Pockets

Have the students empty their pockets. Look for interesting items to use as part of a small story and select three. Divide the class into small groups, and have each group create and act out a small story that involves these items in some important way.

EXERCISE 139

Acting Out the Name

Divide the class into pairs, and give each child a name that suggests a particular type of personality. (*See* the "Characters" section on pages 50–51.) Have the partners act out very simple situations, such as sitting on a park bench or sitting at a lunch counter.

EXERCISE 140

One Sentence Improvisation

Divide the class into groups of two or three students. Give each group a different line to use in an improvisation; one child in the group must say the line during the small story that the group will create and perform.

When explaining this exercise, emphasize that each story must have a beginning, a middle, and an ending. Give each group a short time to create a story and to rehearse their performance.

Here are some suggestions of appropriate lines for this exercise:

It came off in my hand!
I was just standing there.
That's not what I heard at all!
What do you suppose it is?
Is that for me?
I forgot my homework.
What a mess.
Just what I've always wanted!

EXERCISE 141

Last Line Improvisation

Divide the class into groups of two or three students, and give each group a different last line to use in an improvisation. One child in the group must deliver the line as the final line of the skit that the group will perform.

When explaining this exercise, emphasize that each skit must have a beginning, a middle, and an ending. Give each group a short time to create a story and to rehearse their performance.

Here are some suggestions of appropriate last lines for this exercise:

I really couldn't help it.
I wish you had told me before.
You're kidding.
That's why I'm so happy.
I finally got my wish!

EXERCISE 142

First and Last Line Improvisation

Divide the class into groups of two or three students, and give each group two different lines to use in an improvisation. A member of the group must deliver one of the lines as the *first* line of the skit, and the other must be used as the *last* line. Let the members of the group decide which line to use first and which line to use last.

When explaining this exercise, emphasize that the skits the students create and perform must have a beginning, a middle, and an ending. Give each group a short time to create a story and to rehearse their performance.

Here are some suggestions of appropriate first and last lines for this exercise:

Have you ever seen a poisonous snake?
I thought you said it was on Friday.
I think it sounds like fun.
Listen to the music.
We're going camping in a couple of weeks.
I had a funny dream last night.
That wasn't funny.
Who's there?
I'm starting to get cold.
Do you think this house is haunted?
Listen!
Red is my favorite color.
That's not what I heard!
I've got the measles.

EXERCISE 143

Pick a Character, Pick an Action

Create two separate piles of small slips of paper. Write various character types on the slips in one pile and a variety of actions to do on the slips in the other pile.

Have each student pick one slip from each pile. The student must then become the character and perform the action in front of the group.

EXERCISE 144

Faint

Divide the class into pairs. Have each pair work out a situation in which one person tells the other something that makes the latter "faint." (*See* Exercise 46 for directions on the right way to fall.) Then have them switch parts.

EXERCISE 145

Die

Have the students perform this exercise individually. Tell each to think of a way that he or she could "die." Encourage the students to use their imaginations and create their own circumstances. Remind them to use what they learned in Exercise 46 if falling down is part of the way they choose to die.

The ways in which they die can range from very tragic to very funny, but don't conduct this exercise as a guessing game. Here are some ideas students may use for this exercise:

Sneezing to death
Falling off a ladder
Falling off a building
Coughing to death
Being hit by a falling tree
Laughing to death

EXERCISE 146

Three Different Actions— Improvisation

Divide the class into small groups. Give each group three different actions that the group members are to incorporate into an improvisation. Make it clear that each person in the group is responsible for performing an action. The students are free, however, to perform the actions in any order they choose.

Here are some examples of actions that are appropriate for this exercise:

Jump, laugh, crawl
Laugh, fall, cry
Tiptoe, applaud, sneeze
Giggle, jump, die
Whisper, jump up and down, tiptoe

EXERCISE 147

Animals Becoming People

Discuss the different animals at the zoo. Then have the children become different animals. Work on their walks and the noises they make.

When some strong animal types have been developed, give the students some improvisational situations to perform. (*See* the "Actions" section on page 51.) Give the situations an unusual twist by telling the students to perform as human characters who incorporate the specific animal types in the way they look and/or act. For example, put "Mr. Gorilla" and "Miss Mouse" into a situation together, and have them perform as people who have gorilla and mouse traits.

Characters, Places for Characters, Actions for Characters

CHARACTERS

a vampire
a movie star
the silly one
a very old person
the nervous one
the shy one
the lover
the snob
the know-it-all
the grouch

the genius
a cowboy/cowgirl
priest/nun
police officer
the not-too-smart one
a scientist
an opera singer
an elf
a cry-baby
a dancer
a clown
a gangster

Santa Claus
a famous movie star
a professional magician
a person who weighs 300 pounds
a three-year-old
a magic genie
an old witch
a giggler
an acrobat
the generous one
the one who interrupts

PLACES FOR CHARACTERS TO BE

in the movie theatre
in a waiting room
in a library
on the beach
in a zoo
on a boat
on a picnic
on a mountain top
in the woods
in a supermarket
in a classroom
in a swimming pool
on a bus
on a plane

ACTIONS FOR SOLO CHARACTERS

You are . . . .

- doing exercises in front of a mirror.
- walking a dog in the park.
- reading a newspaper on a park bench.

- pushing a baby carriage.
- driving to work in your car.
- playing with your bubble gum.
- combing your hair right after washing it.
- reading a magazine at the beach.
- getting dressed for a party.
- trying to swat a fly with a fly swatter.
- trying to catch your dog.
- blowing up a balloon.
- teaching a dog to climb a ladder.
- doing a dance.
- campaigning for President of the United States.
- demonstrating how to fly without an airplane.
- making up a poem.
- singing a song about yourself.
- showing everyone how to walk a tightrope.
- telling everyone how wonderful and good looking you are.
- demonstrating how to make a carpet fly.
- reacting to having just stepped on a bee.

ACTIONS FOR CHARACTERS IN A GROUP

Together in a stuck elevator.
Eating in a nice restaurant.
Waiting in line at the theatre.
Walking dogs in the park.
Together in the same hospital room.
Sharing a table at a cafe.
Sitting together on a plane.
Sitting in a waiting room.
Waiting for a job interview.
Waiting to see the principal.
Close by each other at the beach.
Sitting together on the bus.

Extending the Activities to Other Areas of the Curriculum

WRITING

Have your students pick a situation from exercises 94, 95, 97, 104, or 106, and compose a letter to the other person explaining the situation.

Let your students pick two characters from Exercise 139 and write a story about how one character changed the other's life—e.g., "How the Gangster Changed the Magic Genie's Life."

Use the one sentence, last line, or first/last line structure from exercise 140, 141, or 142 as the basis for writing a short story.

Challenge your students to describe in writing—in as minute detail as possible—one of the deaths performed in Exercise 145.

ART

Have your students create one of the characters from Exercise 139 in the form of a puppet. They can make sock puppets, stick puppets, puppets made from paper bags, or any other puppet variety they choose. Then let them work in groups, using their puppets to present one of the situations.

In Exercise 145, have your students work in pairs or small groups so that as one person performs a death, the other(s) can sketch it. Encourage the artist(s) to try to capture the mood of the performance.

After Exercise 147, have your students portray themselves as an animal, but this time using a nonperformance art medium—e.g., drawing, painting, creating a collage or clay sculpture.

SOCIAL STUDIES

Use exercises 90, 91, and/or 121 to stimulate a discussion about siblings. Have your students discuss some of the situations in the skits. Ask whether similar situations have happened to them in regard to their own siblings. Ask how they feel about and treat their brothers and sisters. Encourage them to suggest ways they might get along better with their siblings.

Incorporate Exercise 95 into a career education unit by having the students pick a career that interests them and explain why they are better suited to their chosen career than to operating a laundry or another type of business.

SCIENCE

Use Exercise 147 to start some inquiry about animal life. If a student wants to act out "Miss Mouse," for example, have the student first study and (if possible) observe mice. Such study and observation not only increase the student's knowledge but also likely will add depth to the characterization.

PART 5
GROUP DRAMATIZATION

Group dramatization gives the class an opportunity to work together in an improvised play. As an activity, the drama may be developed as far as the class desires. Often students enjoy performing their play for other classes. Exercises 148, 149, and 150 are particularly suited to performing for audiences of younger children. Exercises 151, 152, and 153 give children an opportunity to act out parts of their fantasy world in the context of a group dramatization.

Introducing the Exercises to Your Students

Start by asking your students to recall group dramatic performances they have seen—plays, skits, etc. Ask them, "In what ways do you think people worked together to put on these productions?" Explain that because they have developed so many individual dramatic skills, they are now ready to work together in the following activities that involve dramatizing stories and scenes.

Dramatizing Stories

For the following dramatizations, you may use classic fairy tales and poems or you may draw upon anthologies of stories expressly created for children's creative dramatics. One of the many excellent books of this sort is *Stories for Creative Acting* by C. Robert Kase (published by Samuel French, 1961).

As an alternative approach, you may have the students create original stories for their group dramas. If you are interested in this approach, consider some of the suggestions presented in the writing section of "Extending the Activities to Other Areas of the Curriculum."

For the most part, you may either read or tell the story to the class before assigning parts and assisting the children in planning the improvisation. In exercises 148, 149, and 150, however, you should read the story to the class while the students as a group simultaneously attempt to portray what the story is suggesting.

EXERCISE 148

The Dancing Flowers

Have your students portray this drama as you read it to them.

Once upon a time, there was a beautiful meadow surrounded by large mountains. In the meadow were many flowers. Every day from sunrise to sunset, the flowers would come to life and dance together. (Children portray dancing flowers)

One day a wind came to the meadow and very gently blew the flowers from side to side. (Children portray action of gentle wind and flowers)

The wind grew stronger and stronger until it became a very fierce wind storm. (Children portray the action of the storm)

Big clouds appeared in the sky, and thunder started to make giant crashing sounds. (Children portray thunder)

After the thunder came a lightning storm. Great bolts of lightning came from the sky. (Children portray lightning)

It began to rain very softly. (Children portray soft rain)

The rain stopped, and several huge giants came down from the mountains. The giants had very large feet, and they stepped on the beautiful flowers. (Children portray the action of the giants)

The flowers were left on the ground motionless. (Children portray the lifeless flowers)

Fairies with magic wands appeared from the other side of the mountain. They flew over the meadow and saw what had happened to the flowers. The fairies touched each flower and brought every one of the flowers back to life. (Children portray the action of the fairies and the flowers coming back to life)

As each flower came back to life, it started dancing again. (Children portray dancing flowers; entire story may be repeated)

EXERCISE 149

The Wild Horses

Have your students portray this drama as you read it to them.

Once upon a time, out on the plains, there were many wild horses that ran free all day long. (Children portray horses running)

Some days they would walk around slowly, nibbling at the grass. (Children portray horses nibbling)

Some days they would run so fast and hard that they could hardly stop. (Children portray fast-running horses)

Sometimes it was cold on the plains when the big snowflakes came down. (Children portray snowflakes falling)

Other times it would become windy as storms moved in from the north. (Children portray wind and storms)

One day some cowboys came riding out on the plains. (Children portray cowboys)

The cowboys saw the horses and decided to round them up. (Children portray cowboys rounding up horses)

The cowboys guided the horses back to the ranch. (Children portray cowboys guiding horses)

The people at the ranch decided to tame the wild horses. (Children portray horses bucking and kicking)

Soon the horses calmed down and decided that they liked their new home. They could run free in a large pasture all day long. (Children portray horses running; entire story may be repeated)

EXERCISE 150

The Mean Giants

Have your students portray this drama as you read it to them.

In a deep dark forest a long time ago there were many beautiful animals that played together. There were bears, elephants, kangaroos, and butterflies. (Children portray various animals playing)

There were also some very mean giants who lived in the forest, and they enjoyed chasing and scaring the nice animals. (Children portray giants chasing animals)

One day the god of fire came to the forest and told the animals to find a new place to live. The god of fire said that the giants were so mean that the forest had to be burned down. (Children portray animals leaving the forest)

After the animals left, huge flames started burning the forest. (Children portray flames)

The giants became very frightened, jumped up and down, and promised that they would be nice to the animals. (Children portray frightened giants)

Suddenly it began to rain. The rain came down so hard that it put out the fire. (Children portray rain putting out fire)

All of the animals came hurrying back to the forest. (Children portray returning animals)

The giants were very happy to see the animals, and everyone danced and played together from then on. (Children portray giants and animals playing together)

EXERCISE 151

The Birthday Party

Have the children talk about the fun birthday parties that they have attended. Encourage them to name some of the specific things they did at the parties. Then help them create an improvised party, including entertainment and food.

Tell each child to think of an imaginary gift to bring. After the "gifts" are opened, have the children pass them around for all to enjoy.

EXERCISE 152

Mean and Nice Wishes

This exercise gives children an opportunity to act out a part of their fantasy world that they may be reluctant to talk about. Have each child think of "mean wishes" that he or she would like to see happen, and then let the entire group act out the wishes.

When the class finishes performing all the mean thoughts, have the students transform those thoughts into "good wishes." Using elves with magic wands is usually a good way to bring everything back to normal again.

EXERCISE 153

Magic Elves

Join hands with the students so that everyone forms a large circle. Tell the students that they are all magic elves having magic powers.

One child steps outside the circle. Then the elves decide what they want to turn that child into. When the child is called back into the circle, he or she is told what the elves have decided. All of the children in the circle dance around the child who must act out their magic spell.

When the child finishes acting out the spell, the elves turn the child back into a person again. The exercise is then repeated with another child leaving the circle to have a spell cast on him or her.

Extending the Activities to Other Areas of the Curriculum

WRITING

Have your students write an original story for a group dramatization. You can give them a detailed description of a character or a description of a place, and then let them build a story around the character, the locale, or both.

Your students can adapt stories for dramatization by creating their own scripts. Bring in some real play scripts, and let the children study the format. Then have them work alone or in pairs to create a script for a fairy tale or any story they know.

ART

Have your students illustrate exercises 148, 149, and/or 150 by making a mural that depicts any one of the stories in sequence.

In preparation for the group dramatizations in exercises 148, 149, and 150, let the children design and create their own costumes to wear during the performance.

SOCIAL STUDIES

After doing Exercise 152, ask your students to think of some good wishes for the world (rather than for themselves) and to share their ideas with the class.

After doing Exercise 152, ask your students to think about some famous people (e.g., Mother Teresa, Martin Luther King) who have acted upon their good wishes for others. Then have the students work alone or in groups to research the life and deeds of one of these special people.

SCIENCE

After acting out the weather elements (thunder, lightning, wind, and rain) in Exercise 148, discuss with the class what causes these natural phenomena. Use this discussion as a starting point for some further study about weather and climate.